Castaway Bodies in the Eighteenth–Century English Robinsonade

Mini-Monographs in
Literary and Cultural Studies

VOLUME 5

The titles published in this series are listed at *brill.com/mlcs*

Castaway Bodies in the Eighteenth–Century English Robinsonade

By

Jakub Lipski

BRILL

LEIDEN | BOSTON

The Library of Congress Cataloging-in-Publication Data is available online at https://catalog.loc.gov

Typeface for the Latin, Greek, and Cyrillic scripts: "Brill". See and download: brill.com/brill-typeface.

ISSN 2772-5464
ISBN 978-90-04-69045-5 (paperback)
ISBN 978-90-04-69291-6 (e-book)
DOI 10.1163/9789004692916

Copyright 2024 by Koninklijke Brill NV, Leiden, The Netherlands.
Koninklijke Brill NV incorporates the imprints Brill, Brill Nijhoff, Brill Schöningh, Brill Fink, Brill mentis, Brill Wageningen Academic, Vandenhoeck & Ruprecht, Böhlau and V&R unipress.
All rights reserved. No part of this publication may be reproduced, translated, stored in a retrieval system, or transmitted in any form or by any means, electronic, mechanical, photocopying, recording or otherwise, without prior written permission from the publisher. Requests for re-use and/or translations must be addressed to Koninklijke Brill NV via brill.com or copyright.com.

This book is printed on acid-free paper and produced in a sustainable manner.

Contents

Acknowledgements   VII
List of Figures   VIII

Introduction   1

1   The Castaway's Body in *Robinson Crusoe* and Its Visual Afterlives   12

2   Peter Longueville's *The English Hermit* (1727) and the Myth of the New Adam   32

3   Robert Paltock's *Peter Wilkins* (1751): Mythical Androgyny and Evolutionary Hybridisation   48

4   *The Female American* (1767): a Failed Amazon   68

Coda: Castaway Bodies in the Counter-Canonical Robinsonade   84
1   The Elemental Body in Michel Tournier's *Friday*   85
2   Conquering the Body in Olga Tokarczuk's "The Island"   89
3   Re-reading the Amazonian Myth in J. M. Coetzee's *Foe*   93

Bibliography   99
Index   107

Acknowledgements

Research for this book was funded by the National Science Centre, Poland, as part of the Sonata project number 2020/39/D/HS2/02074 (Poetics of the Body in the English Robinsonade). Pursuing this project was a fascinating adventure, in no small part thanks to the expertise and benevolence of my fellow investigator and companion on this island, Patrick Gill.

At various stages of conceptualising and writing this book I consulted my ideas and material with expert colleagues in the field. I would like to thank Eve Tavor Bannet, Katrin Berndt and Markman Ellis. I am especially grateful to Aneta Lipska and Mary Newbould, who read different versions of the manuscript in its entirety. I was also lucky to receive thorough and constructive feedback from the anonymous readers, which has hopefully made this a better book.

Figures

1   Jules Férat, *Harbert Struggling with Ayerton*, an illustration to Jules Verne's *L'Île mystérieuse* (Paris: J. Hetzel, 1874). Public domain   8

2   John Clark and John Pine, the frontispiece to the first edition of *Robinson Crusoe* (London: W. Taylor, 1719). Courtesy of Beinecke Rare Book and Manuscript Library, Yale University   17

3   Bernard Picart, the frontispiece to the first French edition of *Robinson Crusoe* (Amsterdam: L'Honoré & Chatelain, 1720). Courtesy of Beinecke Rare Book and Manuscript Library, Yale University   18

4   The frontispiece to Thomas Gent's abridgement *The Life and Most Surprizing Adventures of Robinson Crusoe* (London: E. Midwinter, 1722). Courtesy of Beinecke Rare Book and Manuscript Library, Yale University   24

5   George Cruikshank, the frontispiece to the 1831 edition of *Robinson Crusoe* (London: The Shakespeare Press). Private collection   26

6   Walter Paget, the illustration facing page 146 in the 1891 edition of *Robinson Crusoe* (London: Cassell). Public domain. Courtesy of the British Library   27

7   N. C. Wyeth, the frontispiece to the 1920 edition of *Robinson Crusoe* (London: Sampson Low, Marston & Co). Private collection   29

8   The frontispiece to the first edition of Peter Longueville's *The English Hermit* (1727). Courtesy of Beinecke Rare Book and Manuscript Library, Yale University   34

9   Louis-Philippe Boitard, *A Gawrey Extended for Flight*, an illustration to Robert Paltock's *Peter Wilkins* (1751). *The Public Domain Review*   51

10   Louis-Philippe Boitard, *The Front of a Glumm Dressed*, an illustration to Robert Paltock's *Peter Wilkins* (1751). *The Public Domain Review*   52

11   Louis-Philippe Boitard, the illustration of the male hybrid from Ralph Morris's *John Daniel* (1751), from the 1926 edition (London: Holden). Courtesy of the University of Michigan Library, Special Collections Research Center   61

12   Louis-Philippe Boitard, *Nasgigs Engagement with Harlokins General*, an illustration to Robert Paltock's *Peter Wilkins* (1751). *The Public Domain Review*   67

13   The frontispiece to the 1800 edition of *The Female American* (Newburyport: Angier March). Courtesy of Beinecke Rare Book and Manuscript Library, Yale University   75

14   Joanna Concejo, the cover image to Olga Tokarczuk's *Profesor Andrews w Warszawie. Wyspa.* © Joanna Concejo   92

Introduction

Castaway narratives emerging in the wake of Daniel Defoe's *Robinson Crusoe* (1719), so-called Robinsonades, have invariably responded to the ever-changing here and now of the author and the reader alike, safeguarding their position as a fictional form of popular appeal and critical merit. Relatively straightforward in terms of plot – typically moving from some sort of shipwreck and the challenges of castaway experience to survivalist and colonial ventures, confrontation with Others and rescue – these narratives have always demonstrated strong ideological bias, serving as an outlet for, in Rebecca Weaver-Hightower's words, Western "fantasies of conquest",[1] and hence best exemplifying what Markman Ellis labels "the concatenation of novel and empire" throughout the eighteenth century and beyond.[2] The Robinsonade's colonialist agenda, however – whereby an isolated representative of the West, or a group of such representatives, is/are capable of transforming the island and establishing their sovereignty – is a critical construct formed not so much by the genre's reliance on the themes of *Robinson Crusoe*, the imperialist message of which, as we shall see, is far from straightforward,[3] but by its development in the nineteenth century, especially in the Victorian period. Such classic examples of the form as Johann David Wyss's *The Swiss Family Robinson* (1812, English translation 1814), Frederick Marryat's *Masterman Ready* (1841), R. M. Ballantyne's *The Coral Island* (1857) and Jules Verne's *The Mysterious Island* (1874, English translation 1875) redefined the genre as targeted predominantly at a younger audience, for whom exposure to fictional brave Westerners, some considerably younger than the prototypical Crusoe, making new lands their own, constituted part of the larger educational process of social programming. As Joseph Bristow shows, the Robinsonade was one of the key genres in the wider tradition of nineteenth-century narratives of "Empire boys", teaching their juvenile male

---

1   Rebecca Weaver-Hightower, *Empire Islands: Castaways, Cannibals, and Fantasies of Conquest* (Minneapolis: University of *Minnesota* Press, 2007).
2   Markman Ellis, "Novel and Empire", *The Oxford Handbook of the Eighteenth-Century Novel*, ed. J. A. Downie (Oxford: Oxford University Press, 2016), p. 490.
3   This complexity has been competently addressed by Daniel Carey in a "contrapunctual" reading of *Robinson Crusoe*'s colonial message. Carey's study is also a useful survey of post-colonial criticism on *Crusoe*. See Daniel Carey, "Reading Contrapuntally: *Robinson Crusoe*, Slavery, and Postcolonial Theory", *Postcolonial Enlightenment*, ed. Daniel Carey and Lynn Festa (Oxford: Oxford University Press, 2009), pp. 105–136.

© KONINKLIJKE BRILL NV, LEIDEN, 2024 | DOI:10.1163/9789004692916_002

reader to become a "responsible citizen [...] with the future of the world lying upon his shoulders".[4]

In the eighteenth century – the first Robinsonades already began to appear in 1719, shortly after *Crusoe* itself – the politics of conquest was at the core of the genre's ideological programme, too; however, given the early novel's polyphonic constitution, defined by Mikhail Bakhtin as a parallel coexistence of a variety of ideological voices within the novelistic text,[5] it is not surprising that this colonialist message was problematised. As Andrew O'Malley points out, the Robinsonade tradition has "allow[ed] for narratives that imagine subjectivities and identities outside of triumphant, colonial individualism".[6] The example was set by Defoe's *Robinson Crusoe*, where the imperial positivism of the first volume, albeit tentative (as will be shown in Chapter 1), is undermined by the eventual colonial failure in *The Farther Adventures*, and then reasserted again in a quirky call for a crusade against the Islamic world in *Serious Reflections During the Life and Surprising Adventures of Robinson Crusoe*. Indeed, as John Richetti has recently suggested, "ambiguity is a sign of the novel's richness and enduring fascination for readers",[7] and it also characterises its fantasy of conquest, which tends to be taken for granted.

This book is about three eighteenth-century Robinsonades that complicate, though never fully negate, the straightforward imperial message typically associated with this genre. Peter Longueville's *The English Hermit* (1727), Robert Paltock's *Peter Wilkins* (1751) and *The Female American* (1767), by an anonymous author, were all successful and popular Robinsonades at the time, but were somehow forgotten during the Victorian period and have only recently been recovered. By rewriting the myths of the New Adam, the Androgyne and the Amazon, respectively, the three works went beyond, though never completely counter to, the politics of conquest and mastery. Admittedly, the limited material does not allow one to formulate generalist conclusions, and the subsequent focused readings of the selected novels will not aspire to offer a totalising perspective on the eighteenth-century Robinsonade. Nevertheless, a nuanced approach to the multilayered constitution of these narratives will enable insight into the fascinating ideological tensions that these novels

---

4   Joseph Bristow, *Empire Boys: Adventures in a Man's World* (London: HarperCollins Academic, 1991), p. 19.

5   Mikhail Bakhtin, *Problems of Dostoevsky's Poetics*, ed. and trans. Caryl Emerson (Minneapolis: University of Minnesota Press, 1984), pp. 6–7.

6   Andrew O'Malley, "The Progressive Pedagogies of the Modern Robinsonade", *Didactics and the Modern Robinsonade*, ed. Ian Kinane (Liverpool: Liverpool University Press, 2019), p. XIII.

7   John Richetti, Preface to *The Cambridge Companion to "Robinson Crusoe"* (Cambridge: Cambridge University Press, 2018), p. XIII.

INTRODUCTION

exemplify, wavering between conventional imperialism and progressive undertones. As such, rather than telling a general history of the Robinsonade in the eighteenth century, *Castaway Bodies* will aim to reconstruct a micro-tradition with a subversive potential within the wider phenomenon.

The rationale for the selection of this particular set was also due to the fact that the elements of counter-hegemonic message in these Robinsonades nod towards twenty- and twenty-first-century examples of the genre. In the aftermath of World War II, as the various European empires started to disintegrate, and in the context of postmodern thought – especially postcolonial, feminist and ecocritical discourses – the Robinsonade evolved into an anti-imperial form, which explicitly questioned its colonialist heritage and provided a channel for progressive liberal thought.[8] As Ian Kinane has recently demonstrated, the Robinsonade today has preserved its didactic impulse, but as the genre "has begun to move further away from its imperialist, masculinist origins than at any other time in its 300-year heritage", its social programming mostly involves "encoding within its remaining narrative structure progressive counter-ideologies".[9]

The Coda to this book will connect the selected eighteenth-century English novels with twenty- and twenty-first century Robinsonades of various national and linguistic backgrounds. As I will show, while the eighteenth-century examples discussed here were not consistent in subverting the imperial agenda, they opened a space of possibilities for contemporary writers to explore: these ideologically conflicted texts written in the wake of *Robinson Crusoe* anticipate counter-canonical Robinsonades of more recent literary history which, in a sense, book-end the project. By juxtaposing eighteenth-century material with (relatively) contemporary narratives – Michel Tournier's *Vendredi* [*Friday*] (1967), J. M. Coetzee's *Foe* (1986) and Olga Tokarczuk's "Wyspa" ["The Island"] (2001) – I intend to show how the mythical potential of the genre played out more recently and how the Robinsonade continues to maintain its socio-cultural relevance. In doing so, I follow the established critical practice of comparative studies, that of *placing*, defined by Siegbert Prower as "the mutual illumination of several texts, or a series of texts, considered side by side", with the assumption that such juxtapositions of frequently dissimilar

---

8   Contemporary "anti-Crusoes" have been most extensively discussed by Ann Marie Fallon in *Global Crusoes: Comparative Literature, Postcolonial Theory, and Transnational Aesthetics* (Farnham: Ashgate, 2011) and "Anti-Crusoes, Alternative Crusoes: Revisions of the Island Story in the Twentieth Century", *The Cambridge Companion to "Robinson Crusoe"*, ed. John Richetti (Cambridge: Cambridge University Press, 2018), pp. 207–220.

9   Ian Kinane, "The Robinsonade Genre and the Didactic Impulse", *Didactics and the Modern Robinsonade*, ed. Kinane, p. 35.

texts, belonging to various contexts, generate a "greater understanding" of them.[10] Indeed, anachronistically, it is the transformations of the contemporary Robinsonade that have made us sensitive to the potentialities of the genre that go beyond the conventional imperial message. The reason for *what* and *why* are *placed* together, in turn, derives from the common ground of mythical structures that belong to the Robinsonade tradition, which depends for its identity on "remythification", to invoke Eleazar Meletinsky's idea, or "interpreting modern civilisation through mythopoetic eyes".[11] As Laurence Coupe explains, mythical narratives fall into four types: fertility myth, creation myth, deliverance myth and hero myth.[12] The Robinsonade is a unique genre that reconciles these different kinds of narrative: the hero's journey typically becomes a story of new beginning, with the redeemed castaway redefining his or her position within the island environment through a prelapsarian recognition of the natural cycle. While the mythical patterns of *Robinson Crusoe* have been thoroughly examined, with diverse strains of Defoe criticism prioritising the different types,[13] this book will show how the Robinsonade's investment in the mythical is imprinted on the castaway body.

More specifically, the primary focus of my readings of the selected texts will be the ways in which these novels re-enact the myths of the New Adam, the Androgyne and the Amazon through narratives of bodily change. I will argue that the metamorphosing body in the Robinsonade is a space on which the ideological polyphony of the castaway narrative plays out, accepting Juliet McMaster's findings that eighteenth-century novelists were responsive to contemporaneous approaches to the body as a textualised, and thus interpretative, entity, and that they treated its representations as a gateway to character, and to novelistic ideas more generally.[14] McMaster also refers to Barbara Korte's

---

10   Siegbert Prower, *Comparative Literary Studies: An Introduction* (London: Duckworth, 1973), p. 102.

11   Eleazar M. Meletinsky, *The Poetics of Myth*, trans. Guy Lanoue and Alexandre Sadetsky (New York and London: Routledge, 2000), p. 329.

12   Laurence Coupe, *Myth* (London and New York: Routledge, 2009), pp. 1–3.

13   Andrew O'Malley recognises two major schools, reading the Crusoe story as a myth of modern individualism and a founding myth of colonialism, respectively. Andrew O'Malley, *Children's Literature, Popular Culture, and* Robinson Crusoe (Houndmills: Palgrave Macmillan, 2012), p. 51. With respect to the types of mythical narrative under discussion, these two schools reconcile the hero myth and the creation myth. The third strain would be the critical tradition of reading *Robinson Crusoe* as a myth of deliverance, exemplified by G. A. Starr, *Defoe and Spiritual Autobiography* (Princeton: Princeton University Press, 1965).

14   Juliet McMaster, *Reading the Body in the Eighteenth-Century Novel* (Houndmills: Palgrave Macmillan, 2004), p. xiv ff.

INTRODUCTION

claim that "familiar texts may even appear in a new light if their use of body language can be seen more clearly";[15] this holds especially true for narratives of mobility, such as Robinsonades. Writing about the body in eighteenth-century travel writing, Zbigniew Białas coined the phrase "the body wall",[16] highlighting the fact that for the subject in motion the body is the first space where new experiences imprint themselves. In a similar manner, the liminal experiences of the castaway are first and foremost lived through the body, the transformations and metamorphoses of which parallel and elucidate whatever takes place on the island.

The paradigm of spatial discovery, central to the Robinsonade, was therefore not only limited to the world's geographies, but also to the microcosm of the castaway's physicality: indeed, the "age of peregrination", as Elizabeth Bohls labels the eighteenth century,[17] was also the age of anatomical exploration. Nevertheless, in much eighteenth-century fiction, despite emerging realist tendencies, the body was above all an allegorical figure, often conceptualised and/or generalised, rather than particular; it was to be seen, read and interpreted. As Erin M. Goss suggests, literary bodies in the period typically stand for concepts, and as a rule they "are not representational but rhetorical tools that ground and make available components of a conceptual system".[18] Bodies as rhetorical tools become textualised, and as such, Veronica Kelly and Dorothea E. von Mücke point out, the body is both subjected to the changing symbolic orders, an index of "civilisation and discipline", but is also a carrier of "transgression against the hegemonic cultures that it elsewhere serves". To Kelly and von Mücke the "discursive character" of the body, "both disciplined and transgressive", is a source of ambiguity, as it stages a clash between opposing ideological standpoints.[19]

In foregrounding the castaway's physicality, the Robinsonade depends on an inevitable link between the castaway's attempts to control the space of the

---

15 Barbara Korte, *Body Language in Literature* (Toronto: University of Toronto Press, 1997), p. 15.

16 Zbigniew Białas, *The Body Wall: Somatics of Travelling and Discursive Practices* (Frankfurt am Main: Peter Lang, 2006).

17 Elizabeth Bohls, "Age of Peregrination: Travel Writing and the Eighteenth-Century Novel", *A Companion to the Eighteenth-Century English Novel and Culture*, ed. Paula R. Backscheider and Catherine Ingrassia (Oxford: Blackwell, 2005), pp. 97–116.

18 Erin M. Goss, *Revealing Bodies: Anatomy, Allegory, and the Grounds of Knowledge in the Long Eighteenth Century* (Lewisburg: Bucknell University Press, 2013), p. 157.

19 Veronica Kelly and Dorothea E. von Mücke, "Introduction: Body and Text in the Eighteenth Century", *Body and Text in the Eighteenth Century*, ed. Veronica Kelly and Dorothea E. von Mücke (Stanford: Stanford University Press, 1994), p. 4, 6.

island and the space of his or her own body, now confronted with new environmental realities. In this manner, the civilisational patterns imposed on the island are doubled by attempts to protect the body and to accommodate it to new conditions, biological and social. This parallelism reflects a wider conceptual identification of the two spaces in the Robinsonade: the island as the I-land. Writing about this identification, Ian Kinane, following Gilles Deleuze, points out that "the island continues to operate as a symbolic site of individuation and self-reflection",[20] while Brian Stimpson recognises the "metonymic function" of the castaway, whereby the island "becomes a configuration of self".[21] The identification of the castaway's body and the island has also been tellingly captured by some of the visual paratexts of Robinsonades, such as the cover of Tokarczuk's "The Island", on which I will comment in the Coda.

In his attempt to narrow down the definition of the Robinsonade, and distinguish it from other types of castaway or desert island narrative, Maximillian Novak has singled out the theme of spatial conquest, literal and metaphorical, as the crucial generic signal.[22] Seen in this light, the Robinsonade is not only a survival narrative, but first and foremost a story of colonisation. This, of course, points to the dominance of the imperial perspective in Robinsonade criticism. In arguably the most systematic and wide-ranging reading of the genre from this standpoint, Weaver-Hightower writes of the crucial narrative moment when the story of survival becomes a story of conquest: it is the "monarch-of-all-I-survey" scene, in which the castaway ascends a hill and takes a view of the island.[23] Complementing her post-colonial perspective with psychoanalytical theories of incorporation, Weaver-Hightower goes on to argue that spatial conquest is paralleled, or metonymically represented, by the castaway's work on his body (the reading concentrates on conventional male Robinsonades), from atavistic survivalist activities to civilisational self-discipline, comprising repetitive work, mental exercise and sexual abstinence.[24] And, just as work on the land illustrates a transition from nature to (Western) civilisation,

---

20   Ian Kinane, *Theorising Literary Islands* (London: Rowman & Littlefield International, 2017), p. 104. See also Gilles Deleuze, "Desert Islands", *Desert Islands and Other Texts 1953–1974*, by Gilles Deleuze, ed. David Lapoujade, trans. Michael Taormina (Los Angeles: Semiotext(e), 2004), pp. 9–14.

21   Brian Stimpson, "*Insulaire que tu es. Île–*: Valéry, the Robinson Crusoe of the Mind." *Robinson Crusoe: Myths and Metamorphoses*, ed. Lieve Spaas and Brian Stimpson (New York: St. Martin's Press, 1996), pp. 294–315.

22   Novak, *Transformations, Ideology, and the Real in Defoe's* Robinson Crusoe *and Other Narratives*, p. 112.

23   Weaver-Hightower, *Empire Islands*, pp. 1–42.

24   Weaver-Hightower, *Empire Islands*, pp. 59–67.

INTRODUCTION

bodily discipline aims at protecting the castaway from a backward movement, devolution into a "beastly" state, something Weaver-Hightower labels as being "infected" by island "savagery".[25] The Robinsonade tradition abounds in stories of failed colonists, castaways who regressed when in a state of isolation. The prototypical narrative features Alexander Selkirk, one of the direct models for Crusoe, who allegedly forgot how to speak.[26] Ian Watt, writing about Defoe's utopian mentality, notes that he would have been familiar with stories of castaways who, "harassed by fear and dogged by ecological degradation, [...] sank more and more to the level of animals, lost the power of speech, went mad, or died of inanition".[27]

Defoe's Crusoe, through his methodical and systematic physical labour, mental and religious exercise, and the compensation for human conversation he finds with his parrots, succeeds in protecting his body from devolving, as do a number of his literary progeny. In the Robinsonade tradition, however, these stories of success through self-discipline are confronted with shadowy doubles: the progeny of Selkirk, in a sense, or the allegorical warnings about what happens if self-disciplinary measures are not taken. Verne's *The Mysterious Island*, one of the most popular imperial Robinsonades of the nineteenth century, elaborates extensively on this dialectical juxtaposition of castaway bodies. On the one hand, there is a group of American castaways, disciplined military men, who embody the Robinsonade ideal of imperial masculinity. On the other hand, as they extend their colonising ventures to the neighbouring island, they encounter Ayerton, a failed castaway and a failed colonist:

> Indeed it was not an ape, it was a human being, a man. But what a man! A savage in all the horrible acceptation of the word, and so much the more frightful that he seemed fallen to the lowest degree of brutishness!
>
> Shaggy hair, untrimmed beard descending to the chest, the body almost naked except a rag round the waist, wild eyes, enormous hands with immensely long nails, skin the colour of mahogany, feet as hard as if made of horn, such was the miserable creature who yet had a claim to be called a man. But it might justly be asked if there were yet a soul in this body, or if the brute instinct alone survived in it![28]

---

25   Weaver-Hightower, *Empire Islands*, pp, 133–141.

26   "At his first coming on board us, he had so much forgot his Language for want of use, that we could scarce understand him". Woodes Rogers, *A Cruising Voyage around the World*, 2nd ed. (London: Andrew Bell, 1718), p. 129.

27   Ian Watt, *The Rise of the Novel: Studies in Defoe, Richardson and Fielding* (1957; Berkeley and Los Angeles: University of California Press, 2001), p. 88.

28   Jules Verne, *The Mysterious Island* (New York: C. Scribner's Sons, 1930), p. 278.

The Darwinian undertones in Verne's Robinsonade are clear: as Ayerton has devolved, being "infected" by the island, his body is reminiscent of an ape, with the implication that the failed castaway has undergone a backwards-moving process within the framework of the evolutionary paradigm. Jules Férat's illustration of the scene (Figure 1) underlines the racist agenda through

FIGURE 1   Jules Férat, *Harbert struggling with Ayerton*, an illustration to Jules Verne's *L'Île mystérieuse* (Paris: J. Hetzel, 1874)
PUBLIC DOMAIN

INTRODUCTION

its use of light and shade. The light is focused on Harbert's face, emphasising his whiteness, while "mahogany" Ayerton, effectively dark-skinned in the black and white print, seems to have emerged out of nowhere, from the dark recesses of the island. Ayerton's image coheres with the larger panorama of late nineteenth-century discourse concerning progress and degeneration, which were inherently "pre-supposed and counterposed to one another", as Daniel Pick aptly remarks.[29]

The Robinsonades that come under scrutiny in what follows go beyond this dialectic of imperial masculinity and devolution, foregrounding ambiguous bodily transformations that evade straightforward categorisations within the conventional binaries. In this, the complex representations of physicality parallel the equivocal, at times contradictory, political messages of the novels, oscillating between typical colonialist discourse and non-standard, progressive messages. I will provide examples of positively evaluated bodily metamorphoses that complicate the ideal of imperial masculinity, metonymically representing the castaway's life on the island as one that does not fully comply with the imperative of conquest, though it never abandons it completely.

The examples of changing bodies studied here show how the eighteenth-century English Robinsonade was able to problematise the imperial message by revising three myths that are arguably central to the Robinsonade tradition. The myth of the New Adam lies at the core of the Edenic undertones of the Robinsonade. While Novak has argued that Edenic narratives should be distinguished from the Robinsonade, as they do not depend on the motif of spatial conquest for their generic identity,[30] such clear-cut generic boundaries are not always confirmed by the textual complexity of the Robinsonade, with imperial messages frequently disguised as allegories of paradise regained. The figure of the New Adam in the Robinsonade foregrounds a primordial wonder at the environment and its abundance, a new beginning, and a re-enactment of the mythical command to "subdue" the earth (Genesis 1: 28) in a way that underlines a harmonious coexistence between the human subject and other forms of creation, as is the case in Longueville's *The English Hermit*. The Robinsonade's engagement with stories of new beginning also finds its expression in how the genre reworks the myth of the Androgyne. Kinane has argued that the island in the Robinsonade is a heterotopic place; that is, a place where

---

29 Daniel Pick, *Faces of Degeneration: A European Disorder, c. 1848–c. 1914* (Cambridge: Cambridge University Press, 1989), p. 15.

30 Maximillian E. Novak, "Edenic Desires: *Robinson Crusoe*, the Robinsonade, and Utopian Forms", *Transformations, Ideology, and the Real in Defoe's* Robinson Crusoe *and Other Narratives: Finding the "Thing itself"* (Newark: University of Delaware Press, 2015), pp. 111–127.

(according to Michel Foucault) cultural "emplacements" are "simultaneously represented, contested and inverted".[31] As such, Kinane writes, the island is a "malleable" and "conceptually renegotiable space".[32] This holds true for Robinsonade representations of and, more broadly, engagements with sex, sexuality and gender, from Robinson Crusoe's curious asexuality to Henry De Vere Stacpoole's 1908 *Blue Lagoon*, which fictionalises a romantic union of the two sexes in an Edenic setting, and Tokarczuk's representation of sexual hybridisation in "The Island". Paltock's *Peter Wilkins* reworks the myth of the Androgyne in an even more explicit manner by including a mythical story of cosmic origin, including the differentiation of the sexes, thus combining two fundamental mythical structures: creation and the hero's journey. The figure of the Amazon, related to the Androgyne in its foregrounding of hybridity and gender non-essentialism, becomes an archetypal framework for female Robinsonades, where aspects of imperial masculinity are "feminised". As I will show in discussing *The Female American*, the eighteenth-century Robinsonade did not fully explore this potential, and instead featured female castaways who relied in one way or another on their male companions, whether predecessors or redeemers.

Representations of the body are central to the three myths in question. In the Book of Genesis, a subsidiary but crucial narrative thread concerns Adam's growing awareness of his body, not only in terms of how nakedness becomes inscribed with cultural significance, but also how the body is sentenced to disciplinary labour "by the sweat of the brow" and to Thanatotic metamorphosis: "for dust you are and to dust you will return" (Genesis 3: 19). In the Bible, the mortality of Adam's body is redressed by Christ, the New Adam of the New Testament, whose resurrected body transcends material and temporal limitations, not being subject to decay and suffering.[33] The myth of the Androgyne is, in principle, the myth of the human body: its origins, differentiation and metamorphoses. Its complexity features fully in *Peter Wilkins*, along with its Romantic undertones, which go back to Ovid's *Metamorphoses*. The story of Hermaphrodite, the offspring of Aphrodite and Hermes who merged into one with the nymph Salmacis, shows how heterosexual love leads to a complete unity of the bodies: "Both bodies in a single body mix, / A single body with a double sex",[34] an idea that is also present in the Judeo-Christian concept of marriage with man and wife becoming "one flesh" (Genesis 2: 24).

---

31   Michel Foucault, "Of Other Spaces", trans. Jay Miskowiec, *Diacritics* 16.1 (1986): 24.

32   Kinane, *Theorising Literary Islands*, p. 66.

33   Aquinas, sup 82, 1.

34   Ovid, *Metamorphoses* (London: Jacob Tonson, 1717), p. 119.

The Amazon, in turn, displays a body that not only challenges cultural constructions of femininity, but also engenders masculine superiority. When in Homer's *Iliad* King Priam praises his past achievements on the battlefield, he recalls beating *Amazones antianeirai*, that is Amazons that are "manlike" (in Alexander Pope's translation), "man-defying" (William Cowper) or "unsexed" (William Cullen Bryant). These various translators' choices aptly show that the Amazons' gender confusion was, in a sense, pro-active, and constituted a challenge to the masculine order. At the core of this lies the Amazons' legendary self-mutilation, the cutting of the breast to facilitate bow control, and misandric eugenics: the myth of the Amazon uses the hybrid body as a space for projecting socio-political fears.

These three myths, their engagement with the body, and their formal and ideological implications, will constitute the points of convergence between the connected texts belonging to different historical and national contexts, and will provide a common denominator for my comparative readings. As stated before, this book is first and foremost about the potentially subversive tradition within the eighteenth-century English Robinsonade, but the comparisons established in the Coda will create a wider picture of possibilities, showing ways in which the potential of the ideologically polyphonic Robinsonades that emerged in the wake of Defoe's ur-text has come to be explored more recently. The selected twenty- and twenty-first-century examples of the genre rework the very same myths of the body, thus revealing a continuity of the Robinsonade's use of the theme of bodily metamorphosis and its formal and ideological implications.

CHAPTER 1

The Castaway's Body in *Robinson Crusoe* and Its Visual Afterlives

Juliet McMaster, following Barbara Korte's remark about "the limited literary functions with which body language tends to appear in prose fiction before the mid-eighteenth-century",[1] contends that "Defoe, for all his precise information on merchandise and price, is relatively unspecific on physical qualities of appearance, gesture, and expression".[2] While there is no denying that the other novels discussed by McMaster, such as *Tristram Shandy* or *Clarissa*, are much more elaborate in this respect than *Robinson Crusoe*, it is equally problematic to ignore the various meanings that physicality in Defoe's novel conveys: from the embodied workings of the passions, to climactic moments of illness, and finally to the emblematic representations of external appearance. Indeed, Carolyn Houlihan Flynn's earlier observation that "the body [in Defoe] intrudes as material that can only be managed through language self-consciously, often ironically, and always energetically employed"[3] is an apt introduction to the significance of the bodily in Defoe, and more specifically in *Robinson Crusoe*.

The body in *Crusoe* is represented at the intersection of the realist and the allegorical modes, which in general is central to Defoe's pictorial language of description.[4] In other words, what matters is how meticulous Defoe's accounting for the body is, in terms of the verbal-visual effect it creates, but also the allegorical function the word-images perform within the larger network of the novel's ideologies. These networks include discourses on sexuality and cannibalism, which are central to Flynn's study, and Defoe's handling of the mind/soul-body divide, which has been explored by Elizabeth Napier.[5] The following, in turn, concentrates on how the conventional figurations of imperial

---

1   Korte, *Body Language in Literature*, p. 178.
2   McMaster, *Reading the Body in the Eighteenth-Century Novel*, p. XIII.
3   Carolyn Houlihan Flynn, *The Body in Swift and Defoe* (Cambridge: Cambridge University Press, 1990), p. 2.
4   See Jakub Lipski, *Painting the Novel: Pictorial Discourse in Eighteenth-Century English Fiction* (London and New York: Routledge, 2018), pp. 25–41; and Maximillian E. Novak, "Picturing the Thing Itself, or Not: Defoe, Painting, Prose Fiction, and the Arts of Describing", *Eighteenth-Century Fiction* 9.1 (1996): 1–20.
5   Elizabeth R. Napier, *Falling into Matter: Problems of Embodiment in English Fiction from Defoe to Shelley* (Toronto: University of Toronto Press, 2012).

© KONINKLIJKE BRILL NV, LEIDEN, 2024 | DOI:10.1163/9789004692916_003

masculinity that dominated the Victorian Robinsonade are only tentatively established in *Robinson Crusoe*. Whatever the perspective one wishes to adopt when "anatomising" Defoe's castaway, the body, however meticulously sketched, becomes a textual construct embodying ideas rather than an object of scientific enquiry. Defoe does not situate his somatic discourse in the developing fields of natural and medical sciences of his time, perhaps with the exception of the quasi-science of the passions, but rather in the system of cultural signifiers. This can also be observed in other memorable representations of the body in Defoe's fiction, including *Moll Flanders* (1722) and *The Fortunate Mistress* (also known as *Roxana*, 1724), where a changing appearance, from rags to riches, is used as a tool for allegorising the narrative of ups and downs.

Robinson Crusoe's ambiguity in its treatment of the body begins with the question of agency. The generic blend of spiritual autobiography and adventure narrative, fundamental to Defoe's work,[6] leads to a conflicted perspective on Crusoe's fortunes and misfortunes, whereby the castaway is either gracefully saved or methodically saves himself. This conundrum is purposefully never resolved in the novel, and the castaway's body is represented as both passive and active, both an agent of change and an object of the workings of Providence. Crusoe's passiveness comes to the fore at moments of extreme danger, including the memorable scenes of storm and shipwreck, island illness and encounters with others. Defoe's description of Robinson's struggles with the watery element shortly before being stranded on the coast is a particularly vivid example of how skilfully this subject-object dialectic is maintained:

> [...] I could feel my self carried with a mighty Force and Swiftness towards the Shore a very great Way; but I held my Breath, and assisted my self to swim still forward with all my Might. I was ready to burst with holding my Breath, when, as I felt my self rising up [...] it reliev'd me greatly, gave me Breath and new Courage. I was covered again with Water a good while, but not so long but I held it out; and finding the Water had spent it self, and began to return, I strook forward against the Return of the Waves, and felt Ground again with my Feet. I stood still a few Moments to recover Breath, and till the Water went from me, and then took to my Heels, and run with what Strength I had farther towards the Shore. But neither would this deliver me from the Fury of the Sea,

---

6   Artur Blaim has suggested an apt generic formulation for this blend: "adventurous parable". See Artur Blaim, *The Adventurous Parable: Defoe's* Robinson Crusoe (Gdańsk: Wydawnictwo Gdańskie, 1994).

14   CHAPTER 1

which came pouring in after me again, and twice more I was lifted up by
the Waves, and carried forwards as before, the Shore being very flat.[7]

Alternating between the active and the passive grammatical voice, Defoe juxtaposes "a mighty Force" with "all my Might", the erect (standing, running) with
the horizontal (carried, lifted) body,[8] to foreground, I would argue, the perpetual clash of the embodied will and the passive, helpless body, which, in
Napier's words, becomes "a kind of theatre of punishment":[9] it is tossed and
turned, immersed and thrown out, and later, when on the island, feverish and
perfectly immobilised, convulsed with fear and confined in the shelter.

On the other hand, most of the island narrative does indeed feature Crusoe
as disciplined conqueror, transforming the space around him and protecting
himself from "going native", in Weaver-Hightower's words.[10] Defoe highlights
the physicality of labour by playing with the temporal dimension of the narrative: the castaway's repetitive work, such as with the palisade enclosing his
home, goes on for months, becoming a self-disciplining practice with a satisfactory effect:

> this Fence was so strong, that neither Man or Beast could get into it or
> over it: This cost me a great deal of Time and Labour, especially to cut
> the Piles in the Woods, bring them to the Place, and drive them into the
> Earth. (57)

The significance of Crusoe's enclosures has been thoroughly explored in the
relevant criticism. Robert Marzec, for instance, writes about what he terms
"the Crusoe syndrome", that is, "the terror of inhabiting the other space *as* other
[...] until the land is enclosed and transformed."[11] Wolfram Schmidgen, in turn,
suggests a connection between Crusoe's fear of being devoured (by beasts and
cannibals) with the idea of property as a source of protection. Enclosures and
fortifications on the island become a figure of Crusoe's attempts at shielding

---

7   Daniel Defoe, *The Strange Surprizing Adventures of Robinson Crusoe*, ed. Maximillian E.
     Novak, Irving N. Rothman, and Manuel Schonhorn (Lewisburg: Bucknell University Press,
     2020), p. 44. Further references to *Robinson Crusoe* will be parenthetical.
8   Białas discusses the difference between the vertical body (ready to act) and the horizontal
     body symbolising "biological humility". Białas, *The Body Wall*, p. 55.
9   Napier, *Falling into Matter*, p. 5.
10   Weaver-Hightower, *Empire Islands*, pp. 128–137.
11   Robert Marzec, *An Ecological and Postcolonial Study of Literature: From Daniel Defoe to
     Salman Rushdie* (New York: Palgrave, 2007), 3.

THE CASTAWAY'S BODY IN *ROBINSON CRUSOE* AND ITS VISUAL AFTERLIVES   15

his body and function as "extensions of the self".[12] Weaver-Hightower is even more specific, arguing that the enclosure walls are figurations of the skin.[13] The metonymic connection between physical labour with wood and self-discipline is also established by Crusoe's ventures into more advanced carpentry projects:

> If I wanted a Board, I had no other Way but to cut down a Tree, set it on an Edge before me, and hew it flat on either Side with my Axe, till I had brought it to be thin as a Plank, and then dubb it smooth with my Adze. It is true, by this Method I could make but one Board out of a whole Tree, but this I had no Remedy for but Patience, any more than I had for the prodigious deal of Time and Labour which it took me up to make a Plank or Board [...]. (63)

Carefully and laboriously hewn out, the wooden planks become an allegory of discipline, tangible evidence of Crusoe's indomitable labour. The castaway's work on this most basic natural resource is at the same time a way of indicating a link between spatial conquest and body control: the planks and piles help organise and appropriate the land, while the abnormally prolonged and tedious work necessary to produce them, in a manner reminiscent of making a sculpture (hewing off redundant matter), is both a physical and a mental exercise that trains the body and the mind.

While physical labour and the related colonial activities emphasise Crusoe's agency, the potentially degenerating, passive body of a mere survivor, exposed to the various dangers of the island, remains a shadowy presence throughout the novel. It comes to the fore most vividly in the sickness episode, which is both a perfectly logical and plausible representation of what happens to the body in a different climate and a metaphor of the fears of "island infection", broadly understood, as discussed in the Introduction:

> I lay a-Bed all Day, and neither eat or drank. I was ready to perish for Thirst, but so weak, I had not Strength to stand up, or to get my self any Water to drink [...] I fell asleep, and did not wake till far in the Night; when I wak'd, I found my self much refresh'd, but weak, and exceeding

---

12   Wolfram Schmidgen, *Eighteenth-Century Fiction and the Law of Property* (Cambridge: Cambridge University Press, 2004), p. 48.

13   Weaver-Hightower, *Empire Islands*, p. 33. See also Johannes Riquet, *The Aesthetics of Island Space: Perception, Ideology, Geopoetics* (Oxford: Oxford University Press, 2019), 232.

thirsty: However, as I had no Water in my whole Habitation, I was forc'd to lie till Morning, and went to sleep again [...]. (77–78)

Crusoe's fever makes him experience the memorable dream vision, featuring a "dreadful" messenger or personification of Death descending from a "great black Cloud", with a spear in his hand, to kill the castaway. Importantly, the dream features Robinson "Out-side of [his] Wall" (78), vulnerable, implying that the fears of island beasts and cannibals merge with the natural, illness-inspired fear of death. The castaway's vulnerability is also emphasised in the early section of the island narrative, when Crusoe laments:

> All the rest of that Day I spent in afflicting my self at the dismal Circum-stances I was brought to, *viz.* I had neither Food, House, Clothes, Weapon, or Place to fly to, and in Despair of any Relief, saw nothing but Death before me, either that I should be devour'd by wild Beasts, murther'd by Savages, or starv'd to Death for Want of Food. (65)

Crusoe's actions on the island strive to prevent this vision from happening, and his work on the wooden wall is paralleled by his attentiveness to cloth-ing, as depicted by two detailed ekphrastic moments offering fully fledged sketches of Crusoe's appearance. The centrality of these sketches is estab-lished not only by their function within the narrative but also by the fact that they provided the basis for the two best-known frontispieces to the first volume of *Robinson Crusoe*: that by John Clark and John Pine for the first edition (Figure 2), and Bernard Picart's frontispiece to the first French edition published as early as 1720 (Figure 3). David Blewett points out that these two representations "are alike in creating an enduring visual image of the extraordinary figure who so impressed himself upon the European imagination."[14]

A closer focus on what Crusoe looks like and how he is dressed, as con-structed in the text and represented by the engravers, will show how these two sketches differ and underline the ambiguities of Defoe's representation of the body – this time not by questioning Crusoe's agency but by showing that in representing the castaway's survivalist and civilisational activities Defoe was a tentative imperialist. The complexity of the sketches, reconciling, in

---

14   David Blewett, *The Illustration of Robinson Crusoe, 1719–1920* (Gerrards Cross: Colin Smythe, 1995), p. 32.

THE CASTAWAY'S BODY IN *ROBINSON CRUSOE* AND ITS VISUAL AFTERLIVES   17

FIGURE 2   John Clark and John Pine, the frontispiece to the first edition of *Robinson Crusoe* (London: W. Taylor, 1719)
COURTESY OF BEINECKE RARE BOOK AND MANUSCRIPT LIBRARY, YALE UNIVERSITY

FIGURE 3   Bernard Picart, the frontispiece to the first French edition of *Robinson Crusoe* (Amsterdam: L'Honoré & Chatelain, 1720)
COURTESY OF BEINECKE RARE BOOK AND MANUSCRIPT LIBRARY, YALE UNIVERSITY

THE CASTAWAY'S BODY IN *ROBINSON CRUSOE* AND ITS VISUAL AFTERLIVES   19

a sense, aspects of imperial masculinity with the bodily grotesque, will subsequently serve as the immediate background for the quirky castaway narratives analysed in the following chapters, while the focus on the visual afterlives of Crusoe's physicality will trace some of the crucial steps in the formation of the ideal of imperial masculinity that Defoe's castaway came to embody irrespective of the original textual polyphony. These later representations of Crusoe in visual culture do not offer a direct context for the metamorphoses of the body in the selected eighteenth-century Robinsonades, but they help to reconstruct relevant aspects of the popular reception of Defoe's novel as colonial allegory that the non-standard narratives of the eighteenth century problematised, and that the more recent counter-canonical fictions subverted.

The first sketch in Defoe's text (represented by Picart), tellingly enough, is introduced when Robinson has already made himself at home on the island, has created a stand-in "family" (of animals) to entertain himself, and has yet to be thrown off-balance by the footprint. It is then, in a way, an emblematic summary of the toils of a successful castaway, who enjoys a position of undisputed power. However, Defoe problematises Crusoe's hegemony by introducing irony and good-natured humour in the ekphrastic passage, which deserves to be quoted in full:

> [...] had any one in *England* been to meet such a Man as I was, it must either have frightened them, or rais'd a great deal of Laughter; and as I frequently stood still to look at my self, I could not but smile at the Notion of my travelling through *Yorkshire* with such an Equipage, and in such a Dress: Be pleas'd to take a Sketch of my Figure as follows.
>
> I had a great high shapeless Cap, made of a Goat's Skin, with a Flap hanging down behind, as well to keep the Sun from me, as to shoot the Rain off from running into my Neck; nothing being so hurtful in these Climates, as the Rain upon the Flesh under the Cloaths.
>
> I had a short Jacket of Goat-Skin, the Skirts coming down to about the middle of the Thighs; and a Pair of open-knee'd Breeches of the same, the Breeches were made of the Skin of an old *He-goat*, whose Hair hung down such a Length on either Side, that like *Pantaloons* it reach'd to the middle of my Legs; Stockings and Shoes I had none, but had made me a Pair of some-things, I scarce know what to call them, like Buskins to flap over my Legs, and lace on either Side like Spatter-dashes; but of a most barbarous Shape, as indeed were all the rest of my Cloaths.
>
> I had on a broad Belt of Goat's-Skin dry'd, which I drew together with two Thongs of the same, instead of Buckles, and in a kind of a Frog on either Side of this. Instead of a Sword and a Dagger, hung a little Saw and

a Hatchet, one on one Side, one on the other. I had another Belt not so broad, and fasten'd in the same Manner, which hung over my Shoulder; and at the End of it, under my left Arm, hung two Pouches, both made of Goat's-Skin too; in one of which hung my Powder, in the other my Shot: At my Back I carry'd my Basket, on my Shoulder my Gun, and over my Head a great clumsy ugly Goat-Skin Umbrella, but which, after all, was the most necessary Thing I had about me, next to my Gun. As for my Face, the Colour of it was really not so *Moletta*, like as one might expect from a Man not at all careful of it, and living within nineteen Degrees of the *Equinox*. My Beard I had once suffer'd to grow till it was about a Quarter of a Yard long; but as I had both Scissars and Razors sufficient, I had cut it pretty short, except what grew on my upper Lip, which I had trimm'd into a large Pair of *Mahometan* Whiskers, such as I had seen worn by some *Turks*, who I saw at *Sallé*; for the *Moors* did not wear such, tho' the *Turks* did; of these Mustachoes, or Whiskers, I will not say they were long enough to hang my Hat upon them; but they were of a Length and Shape monstrous enough, and such as in *England* would have pass'd for frightful. (124–125)

The meticulous presentation of the various elements making up Crusoe's clothing and look accords with Defoe's poetics of detailed description, which is also prominent in the reporting of the colonising ventures of the castaway. The relationship between civilisational and bodily discourse, then, is established by formal means, with the same language used for nuanced representations of the castaway's homes, stores and enclosures, and himself. But the parallel depends on contrast: just as the island is subject to transformations orchestrated by Crusoe, the body of the castaway must be protected against changes that might take place under the influence of the island, that is, against being "infected" by the island. This is rendered by the foregrounding of the gun and the umbrella – the two most "necessary things" Robinson possesses. Just as the gun facilitates Crusoe's conquest, so the umbrella saves his face from going "*Moletta*", with clearly racist undertones. But the umbrella, paradoxically, is not a symbol of urbanity, as the southern European tradition of using it against the sun did not, for obvious climatic reasons, take root in late seventeenth-century England, and Crusoe admits to having modelled his on those he saw in Brazil (113). So, just as his taking control of the island is facilitated by what he manages to reclaim from the shipwreck – the remnants of Western civilisation – he does not "go native" through an inventive negotiation of what he learns elsewhere.

a sense, aspects of imperial masculinity with the bodily grotesque, will subsequently serve as the immediate background for the quirky castaway narratives analysed in the following chapters, while the focus on the visual afterlives of Crusoe's physicality will trace some of the crucial steps in the formation of the ideal of imperial masculinity that Defoe's castaway came to embody irrespective of the original textual polyphony. These later representations of Crusoe in visual culture do not offer a direct context for the metamorphoses of the body in the selected eighteenth-century Robinsonades, but they help to reconstruct relevant aspects of the popular reception of Defoe's novel as colonial allegory that the non-standard narratives of the eighteenth century problematised, and that the more recent counter-canonical fictions subverted.

The first sketch in Defoe's text (represented by Picart), tellingly enough, is introduced when Robinson has already made himself at home on the island, has created a stand-in "family" (of animals) to entertain himself, and has yet to be thrown off-balance by the footprint. It is then, in a way, an emblematic summary of the toils of a successful castaway, who enjoys a position of undisputed power. However, Defoe problematises Crusoe's hegemony by introducing irony and good-natured humour in the ekphrastic passage, which deserves to be quoted in full:

> [...] had any one in *England* been to meet such a Man as I was, it must either have frightened them, or rais'd a great deal of Laughter; and as I frequently stood still to look at my self, I could not but smile at the Notion of my travelling through *Yorkshire* with such an Equipage, and in such a Dress: Be pleas'd to take a Sketch of my Figure as follows.
>
> I had a great high shapeless Cap, made of a Goat's Skin, with a Flap hanging down behind, as well to keep the Sun from me, as to shoot the Rain off from running into my Neck; nothing being so hurtful in these Climates, as the Rain upon the Flesh under the Cloaths.
>
> I had a short Jacket of Goat-Skin, the Skirts coming down to about the middle of the Thighs; and a Pair of open-knee'd Breeches of the same, the Breeches were made of the Skin of an old *He-goat*, whose Hair hung down such a Length on either Side, that like *Pantaloons* it reach'd to the middle of my Legs; Stockings and Shoes I had none, but had made me a Pair of some-things, I scarce know what to call them, like Buskins to flap over my Legs, and lace on either Side like Spatter-dashes; but of a most barbarous Shape, as indeed were all the rest of my Cloaths.
>
> I had on a broad Belt of Goat's-Skin dry'd, which I drew together with two Thongs of the same, instead of Buckles, and in a kind of a Frog on either Side of this. Instead of a Sword and a Dagger, hung a little Saw and

a Hatchet, one on one Side, one on the other. I had another Belt not so broad, and fasten'd in the same Manner, which hung over my Shoulder; and at the End of it, under my left Arm, hung two Pouches, both made of Goat's-Skin too; in one of which hung my Powder, in the other my Shot: At my Back I carry'd my Basket, on my Shoulder my Gun, and over my Head a great clumsy ugly Goat-Skin Umbrella, but which, after all, was the most necessary Thing I had about me, next to my Gun. As for my Face, the Colour of it was really not so *Moletta*, like as one might expect from a Man not at all careful of it, and living within nineteen Degrees of the *Equinox*. My Beard I had once suffer'd to grow till it was about a Quarter of a Yard long; but as I had both Scissars and Razors sufficient, I had cut it pretty short, except what grew on my upper Lip, which I had trimm'd into a large Pair of *Mahometan* Whiskers, such as I had seen worn by some *Turks*, who I saw at *Sallé*; for the *Moors* did not wear such, tho' the *Turks* did; of these Mustachoes, or Whiskers, I will not say they were long enough to hang my Hat upon them; but they were of a Length and Shape monstrous enough, and such as in *England* would have pass'd for frightful. (124–125)

The meticulous presentation of the various elements making up Crusoe's clothing and look accords with Defoe's poetics of detailed description, which is also prominent in the reporting of the colonising ventures of the castaway. The relationship between civilisational and bodily discourse, then, is established by formal means, with the same language used for nuanced representations of the castaway's homes, stores and enclosures, and himself. But the parallel depends on contrast: just as the island is subject to transformations orchestrated by Crusoe, the body of the castaway must be protected against changes that might take place under the influence of the island, that is, against being "infected" by the island. This is rendered by the foregrounding of the gun and the umbrella – the two most "necessary things" Robinson possesses. Just as the gun facilitates Crusoe's conquest, so the umbrella saves his face from going *"Moletta"*, with clearly racist undertones. But the umbrella, paradoxically, is not a symbol of urbanity, as the southern European tradition of using it against the sun did not, for obvious climatic reasons, take root in late seventeenth-century England, and Crusoe admits to having modelled his on those he saw in Brazil (113). So, just as his taking control of the island is facilitated by what he manages to reclaim from the shipwreck – the remnants of Western civilisation – he does not "go native" through an inventive negotiation of what he learns elsewhere.

Crusoe in general pays considerable attention to clothing, from the items he wore when he was shipwrecked, to those he found on the two wrecks he searched, to those he crafted himself. His attentiveness to what he wears is, of course, commonsensical, but clothes in the eighteenth-century novel typically gained in metaphorical significance as belonging to the index of the self, which will be elaborated upon in the subsequent chapters. This idea is succinctly captured by Jessica Munns and Penny Richards in the title of their collection of essays, *The Clothes that Wear Us*;[15] it inverts agency and implies the formative function of garments, which blend with the body to construct an image of self. When Crusoe meets Friday and begins to "mould" the other according to his standards, one of his first decisions, ridiculously enough, is to give him clothes, "for which he seem'd very glad, for he was stark naked" (172). Why would Friday, perfectly accustomed to being naked, be "very glad" about receiving clothes? To a twenty-first-century reader, this reads like an imperial projection of colonial mimicry that chimes with Friday's later "they willing love learn", inviting Crusoe to bestow upon the native people the "blessings" of religious, culinary and linguistic education that Friday has received from the castaway. However, in the system of eighteenth-century fiction, Friday's new clothes (just like his new name) are also an allegory of a new beginning, a quasi-bodily change, and, perhaps, an attempt to protect the "Sweetness and Softness of an *European* in his Countenance" and to prevent his "agreeable", "dun olive Colour" from becoming "an ugly yellow nauseous tawny" (171–172).[16]

That said, there is little in this character sketch that brings to mind the later ideal of imperial masculinity. Even the overgrown facial hair, which became iconic in the Robinsonade tradition and could be taken to symbolise, as Weaver-Hightower argues, the imperial father figure, is treated light-heartedly here, with an element of bodily grotesque – the mixture of laughter (hanging a hat upon whiskers) and monstrosity ("monstrous", "frightful"). The foreign import (that is, the umbrella), too, undermines the imperial message of the character sketch, as if implying that it is inevitable for travels and intercultural encounters to imprint themselves on the "body wall", to use Białas's concept.

---

15   Jessica Munns and Penny Richards (eds.), *The Clothes that Wear Us: Essays on Dressing and Transgressing in Eighteenth-Century Culture* (Newark and London: University of Delaware Press, 1999).

16   As Suvir Kaul accurately puts it, the sketch of Friday's endearing looks is "suitably developed against a checklist of offending non-European facial and epidermal features", such as the "tawny" colour. Suvir Kaul, *Eighteenth-Century British Literature and Postcolonial Studies* (Edinburgh: Edinburgh University Press, 2009), p. 74.

As Roxann Wheeler observes, this character sketch of Crusoe, when juxtaposed with remarks upon Friday's "Europeanness", presents readers with a complex dynamic whereby the bodies of the changed castaway and the curiously homely native man create "a pattern of partially collapsed boundaries of difference".[17]

While Napier's assertion that Crusoe depicts his own body as either "helpless" (as a theatre for punishment) or "absurd" (in character sketches) might be too restrictive,[18] Defoe clearly plays with Robinson's dressed body to deprive the coloniser of imperial splendour. Given the popularity of Picart's frontispiece, its numerous reprints across Europe, and the fact that it was not unusual for Continental translators to rely on the French edition, it is intriguing that it was this image of Crusoe that had a profound impact on the Continental reception of Defoe's novel, rather than the frontispiece by Clark and Pine, which is more straightforward in depicting Crusoe's imperial masculinity, and became the canonical frontispiece used in numerous English editions, authorised and unauthorised, in the eighteenth century and beyond. In Robert Folkenflik's words, it was "arguably the most iconic book illustration of an eighteenth-century novel", and provided a model for Picart (though the differences are now apparent) and other illustrators.[19] It shows the castaway bracing himself for the possible defence of "his" island against newcomers, who, as he rightly predicts, might prove villains:[20]

> I fitted my self up for a Battle, as before; though with more Caution, knowing I had to do with another kind of Enemy than I had at first: I order'd *Friday* also, who I had made an excellent Marks-Man with his Gun, to load himself with Arms: I took my self two Fowling-Pieces, and I gave him three Muskets; my Figure indeed was very fierce; I had my formidable

---

17   Roxann Wheeler, *The Complexion of Race: Categories of Difference in Eighteenth-Century British Culture* (Philadelphia: University of Pennsylvania Press, 2000), p. 80.

18   Napier, *Falling into Matter*, p. 21.

19   Robert Folkenflik, "The Rise of the Illustrated English Novel to 1832", *The Oxford Handbook of the Eighteenth-Century Novel*, ed. J. A. Downie (Oxford: Oxford University Press, 2016), p. 313.

20   David Blewett does not agree with this reading of the frontispiece, arguing that this is a phantom ship of Crusoe's mind. He claims that if the scene were showing Crusoe waiting to "welcome" the English ship, then the castaway would be looking at it and would wear a different facial expression. I would argue that Crusoe's look too closely resembles how he is described in the scene in the novel, including the exact number and type of weapons and his dress, to support this argument. That Crusoe is not looking at the ship could easily be explained by the generic shape of the frontispiece: the en-face portrait. See Blewett, *The Illustration of Robinson Crusoe*, pp. 27–30.

Goat-Skin Coat on, with the great Cap I have mention'd, a naked Sword by my Side, two Pistols in my Belt, and a Gun upon each Shoulder. (212)

In contrast with the previous sketch, this account is clearly less verbose, and the poetics of enumeration, unambiguously, is adopted here precisely to account for the weapons Crusoe carries. The use of adjectives is monological – "fierce", "formidable", "great" – as the narrative context of the description, Crusoe's "battle" to protect the land, leaves little room for ideological polyphony. In Clark and Pine's engraving, in turn, the bodily grotesque of the earlier sketch, and Picart's depiction of it, translates into a gravity of expression that, even if not necessarily responsive to the mention of "fierceness" in the text, can be read as manifesting the archetype of the colonial father, not least because of the stately facial hair.

In sum, while there is room for the ideal of imperial masculinity in Defoe's polyphonic text, it is counterbalanced by more complex representations of the body: from mentions of passivity, weakness and illness to the use of irony and the bodily grotesque. As I have argued elsewhere, Defoe typically resorted to fully fledged ekphrastic moments in the context of scenes that had a crucial significance for the ideological, and indeed allegorical, shape of his narratives.[21] His pictorial language with reference to what Crusoe looks like deserves special attention in as much as it foregrounds Defoe's equivocal embodiment of the castaway, a quality that, arguably, corresponds to the wider panorama of ambiguities and seeming inconsistencies across the Crusoe trilogy. That said, the vibrant afterlife of *Crusoe* in Britain until the final decades of the eighteenth century, with dozens of new editions, abridged and pirated versions published with considerable regularity, typically promoted, through the frontispiece, the monological variant of the castaway's imperial body depicted by Clark and Pine, as exemplified by the cheap woodcut in the infamous abridgement by Thomas Gent (Figure 4). The form of the woodcut, simplifying the careful delineation of the engraving, is a kind of testimony to the process of simplification and monologisation that the *Crusoe* story was undergoing through its abridgements.

More advanced, individualised pieces revealing the influence of this iconic engraving appeared from the 1780s onwards, and include works by Mather Brown, Thomas Stothard and Charles Ansell.[22] This sentimental or

---

21   See Lipski, *Painting the Novel*, pp. 32–39.

22   See David Blewett, "The Iconic Crusoe: Illustrations and Images of *Robinson Crusoe*", *The Cambridge Companion to "Robinson Crusoe"*, ed. John Richetti (Cambridge: Cambridge University Press, 2018), pp. 166–170.

FIGURE 4 The frontispiece to Thomas Gent's abridgement *The Life and Most Surprizing Adventures of Robinson Crusoe* (London: E. Midwinter, 1722)
COURTESY OF BEINECKE RARE BOOK AND MANUSCRIPT LIBRARY, YALE UNIVERSITY

pre-Romantic interlude in depicting the castaway preserves the key aspects of Clark and Pine's representation, while smoothing away its rusticity and aligning it with the standards of late eighteenth-century politeness and sensibility. For example, Ansell's Crusoe is endowed with gentlemanly qualities, such as surprisingly well-ordered facial hair, while Stothard's and Brown's suggest a certain degree of melancholic pensiveness. These renditions correspond to the inherent, natural nobility that the Friday figures display, captured through allusions to classical sculpture's iconography of nakedness. The implication is clear: the "noble savage" requires a gentle coloniser, but a coloniser nevertheless.[23]

As noted before, the ideal of imperial masculinity dominated the nineteenth-century afterlives of *Crusoe*. A key moment in the history of its visual reception is George Cruikshank's set of illustrations to the 1831 edition. They create their own narrative, from Young Crusoe's dialogue with his father opening volume 1, to a battle against a horde of Tartars closing volume 2, which alludes to the bildungsroman tradition, and emphasises, by the conceptual move from home-leaving to battle, Crusoe's development from a young boy to a fierce imperialist. The frontispiece (Figure 5) re-stages Clark and Pine's Crusoe, going back in narrative chronology to the encounter with Friday, thus juxtaposing the two scenes where the representations of body – the castaway's and the other's – fuel the novel's colonial undertones. Admittedly, Cruikshank's iconography supports these undertones in a manner that foreshadows the Robinsonade's blend of didacticism and imperial social programming in the ensuing Victorian period. Fully dressed, from head to toe, with a cap that highlights his erect position, Christ-like Crusoe opens his arms to show his good intentions, thus inviting crouched and naked Friday to rise and follow him, with a far less welcoming alternative option silently signalled by the naked corpse in the background.

Popular representations of the castaway in the Victorian period, such as John Gilbert's, Phiz's, and J. D. Watson's, typically elaborated on this strain of representing Crusoe's body, largely overlooking Defoe's original double voice, and instead treating Cruikshank as a central point of reference. Even though, as Blewett shows through his discussion of Ernest Griset's set of 1869, there was room for idiosyncrasies, the 1890s, the "golden decade in English book illustration" and at the same time "a sustained period of empire-building", framed the *Crusoe* story as a reading for adventure-thirsty young boys, emphasising

---

23   See David Blewett, "Robinson Crusoe, Friday, and the Noble Savage: The Illustration of the Rescue of Friday Scene in the Eighteenth Century", *Man and Nature / L'homme et la nature*, 5, 1986, pp. 29–49. https://doi.org/10.7202/1011850ar.

FIGURE 5   George Cruikshank, the frontispiece to the 1831 edition of *Robinson Crusoe* (London: The Shakespeare Press)
PRIVATE COLLECTION

warfare and nationalist sentiments,[24] as exemplified by Walter Paget's 1891 "I was then obliged to shoot" scene (Figure 6). Such representations of Crusoe, as Martin Green puts it in his classic study, were "a central mythic expression" of Empire and became an implicit "call to young men to go out to expand [it]".[25]

24   Blewett, "The Iconic Crusoe", pp. 177–178.
25   Martin Green, *Dreams of Adventure, Deeds of Empire* (New York: Basic Books, 1979), p. 83.

THE CASTAWAY'S BODY IN *ROBINSON CRUSOE* AND ITS VISUAL AFTERLIVES   27

FIGURE 6   Walter Paget, the illustration facing page 146 in the 1891 edition of *Robinson Crusoe* (London: Cassell)
PUBLIC DOMAIN. COURTESY OF THE BRITISH LIBRARY

In time, Crusoe's original attentiveness to the protection of the skin yielded to a fantasy of what might be termed "muscular imperialism", foregrounding the castaway as an embodiment of idealised masculinity. In his series of 1920 colour plates, N. C. Wyeth, who also illustrated Verne's *The Mysterious Island* in a similar manner,[26] represents the castaway as an attractive man, for whom island isolation becomes an opportunity significantly to improve his looks and prowess. The illustrations that depict Crusoe at work or in battle reveal his strained muscles through purposely rolled up sleeves, unbuttoned shirt and short trousers. Representing the scene with Crusoe on the raft, in turn, Wyeth renders the castaway half naked, displaying his muscular torso in a posture of dominance and control (Figure 7). Not without a reason was this scene used as a frontispiece to the edition, foregrounding the admirable change of physicality prompted by labour and discipline, rather than Crusoe's protection of his body, as the Clark and Pine image does. This muscular ideal will be further elaborated upon in Chapter 2 as a central aspect of castaway Peter Quarll's bodily metamorphosis on the island.

This is also how Robinson Crusoe is represented in an early Hollywood adaptation, albeit very loose, titled *Mr. Robinson Crusoe* of 1932. Played by Douglas Fairbanks, who had by that time starred as such embodiments of heroic masculinity as Zorro (1920), D'Artagnan (1921) and Robin Hood (1922), Robinson Crusoe, now proudly displaying part of his Tarzan-like torso and openly alluding to scenes from Fairbanks's *Robin Hood*, is an artificial construct created by protagonist Steve Drexel, who strands himself on an island to prove that he can recreate New York City there. In a manner characteristic of classical Hollywood cinema, the film plays with open and latent bodily display – Crusoe's, his encountered female companion's (dubbed Saturday), and the unequivocally stereotypical others' – and combines the politics of spatial, sexual and racial conquest, as rendered in one item from the film's promotional materials.[27]

In its treatment of the body, *Mr. Robinson Crusoe* also relies on the mythical, with the opening two title cards announcing:

> From the time Adam and Eve were banished from the Garden of Eden, man has vainly sought to find solace, comfort and earthly pleasures in an artificial world of his own creation. Down through the ages has come that eternal heritage – the urge in every man to turn his back on so-called civilization, to get back to nature and revel in the glories and freedom of a primitive paradise.[28]

---

26   See Weaver-Hightower, *Empire Islands*, p. 5.

27   Poster to *Mr. Robinson Crusoe*. United Artists, 1932, https://www.imdb.com/title /tt0023243/mediaviewer/rm1013843456/?ref_=tt_md_9.

28   *Mr. Robinson Crusoe*, 01:00, https://archive.org/details/mr_robinson_crusoe/mr._robin son_crusoe.mp4.

FIGURE 7   N. C. Wyeth, the frontispiece to the 1920 edition of *Robinson Crusoe* (London: Sampson Low, Marston & Co)
PRIVATE COLLECTION

The re-enactment of the myth, a narrative of paradise regained, involves a reduction of the sartorial, again very much like in Longueville's *The English Hermit* and largely in contrast to Defoe's *Robinson Crusoe*. With positively valued "primitiveness" indicating freedom from civilisational constraints, Fairbanks's Crusoe allows his dress to disintegrate gradually, allowing his "natural", Edenic masculinity to surface. More recently, this bodily change has been powerfully rendered in Robert Zemeckis's *Cast Away* (2000), where a leap in story-time is signalled by Chuck Noland's transition from a chubby Yankee dressed in a T-shirt to a naked and muscular king of the island, while the sexuality of bodily "primitivism" is invariably emphasised in television shows exploring the Robinsonade myth.[29]

Admittedly, the outline presented of Crusoe's visual afterlives up to the early twenty-first century is far from comprehensive, but its role has been to mark crucial moments in the process of Defoe's castaway becoming an embodiment of imperial masculinity in the popular imagination, largely separate from its original textual background. A number of these representations monologise the novel's somatic language, not only with respect to Robinson but also in their depictions of Friday. The first encounter between the castaway and the other in the novel, including the memorable presentation of Friday's appearance and his iconic posture with Robinson's foot on the native man's head, creates a meaningful aesthetic and ideological tension that modern criticism of Defoe has successfully explored by pointing to the limits of a straightforward, colonial interpretation.[30] Monological representations of the intercultural encounter, such as Paget's or Wyeth's, foreground the imperial racist agenda using the iconography of warfare and adventure, which is in no way counterbalanced, as it is in Defoe, by an ideological tentativeness and a poetics of ambiguity.

Ever since James Joyce famously labelled Crusoe "the true symbol of the British Empire" and "the true prototype of the British colonist",[31] much critical thought has been devoted to the unquestionable imperial meanings of Defoe's novel. Accordingly, the Robinsonade has typically been perceived as a genre of colonial fantasy and appropriate socio-educational programming (when analysed as material for younger audiences). While the justness of such readings of Defoe's novel and the literary tradition that it sparked will not be argued against in what follows, my aim will be to show how the selected eighteenth-century Robinsonades managed to elaborate on what might be termed Defoe's imperial tentativeness. None of this is present in Joyce's assessment, which simplifies Defoe's narrative, suggesting that the prototypical colonist was able to

---

29 See Barney Samson, *Desert Islands and the Liquid Modern* (Cham: Palgrave Macmillan, 2020), pp. 119–131.

30 For an overview of critical perspectives on the encounter, see Maximillian E. Novak, Irving R. Rothman and Manuel Schonhorn, "Introduction" to Daniel Defoe, *The Life and Strange Surprizing Adventures of Robinson Crusoe* (Lewisburg: Bucknell University Press, 2020), p. xxxix.

31 James Joyce, "Daniel Defoe", Robinson Crusoe, by Daniel Defoe, ed. Michael Shinagel (New York and London: Norton, 1994), p. 323.

conquer the land singlehandedly and with little at his disposal – "in his pocket a knife and a pipe". Very much like Jean-Jacques Rousseau's earlier reading of the novel, praising Crusoe's ingenuity despite being "alone" and "deprived of the assistance of his kind and the instruments of all the arts",[32] Joyce's imperial perspective on the myth smooths away the original ambiguities: in this case, the broader narrative of how the Providentially retrieved tools and remnants of his own civilisation helped him sustain himself.

In the Robinsonades discussed in the subsequent chapters, Defoe's textual ambiguities are given a relevant imitative treatment. This, I argue, can best be seen in how the novels engage with the castaway's body, especially when it complicates the ideal of imperial masculinity that was established not so much by Defoe's novel as by its popular, visual afterlives. As the said ideal of the body, derived, in a sense, from Defoe's second sketch of the castaway and the Clark and Pine frontispiece, has been given relatively extensive critical attention, most notably in Weaver-Hightower's authoritative study, my focus will be on non-standard representations of physicality, elaborating on the problematic aspects of Robinson's appearance in the first sketch, depicting a body that alienates, aesthetically and ideologically, through difference.

Crusoe's double-voice in representing the castaway's body can also be read in the Bakhtinian terms of the clash of the classical and the grotesque body. The former, Bakhtin writes, is "a strictly completed, finished product", endowed with a distinct identity, clearly separated from other bodies.[33] Bakhtin's original point of reference was Renaissance visual art and its reliance on the classical models of beauty, but the metaphor can well be extended to encompass representations of the complete body understood more broadly – as an emblematic carrier of specific messages produced at the crossover of aesthetics and ideology. On the other hand, the grotesque body is porous and not finished; it is a body that undergoes constant metamorphoses and is never completely separate from its social and natural environments. For Bakhtin, such representations were part of the broader aesthetic and ideological concept of grotesque realism, and while the first sketch of Crusoe can hardly be seen as part of Defoe's venture into the carnivalesque, it does manifest the tinge of humorous deformity and a dynamically patchwork constitution showing the imprint of the environment. As such, Crusoe's grotesque body foreshadows the quirky set of non-standard castaway bodies analysed in what follows.

---

32   Jean-Jacques Rousseau, *Emile, or On Education*, ed. and trans. Christopher Kelly and Allan Bloom (Hanover, NH: University Press of New England, 2010), 332.

33   Mikhail Bakhtin, *Rabelais and His World*, trans. Hélène Iswolsky (Bloomington and Indianapolis: Indiana University Press, 1984), p. 29.

CHAPTER 2

Peter Longueville's *The English Hermit* (1727) and the Myth of the New Adam

The English Hermit by Peter Longueville was an extremely popular Robinson-ade in the eighteenth century and is now gradually re-establishing itself as a text that merits critical attention.[1] According to the *English Short Title Cata-logue*, by the end of the eighteenth century the novel had gone into 36 edi-tions, including popular abbreviations, such as the 1795 *New Robinson Crusoe*, so titled to capitalise on the popularity of J. H. Campe's *Robinson der Jüngere*, translated into English as *The New Robinson Crusoe*. Next to nothing is known about the author, but his Preface to *The English Hermit* reveals both authorial self-confidence and intertextual competence. As a framing device, the Pref-ace makes sure the novel exploits the already considerable fame of *Robinson Crusoe*, which by 1727 had not only been followed by Defoe's two sequels but had also been abridged, pirated, translated and reissued a number of times. In doing so, however, Longueville dubs *Crusoe* and Defoe's other works as "vulgar", which is the reason why they "had their Admirers among the lower Rank of Readers".[2] He similarly distances himself from the other successful imaginary voyage of the period – Jonathan Swift's *Gulliver's Travels* (1726) – in this case because it is a work for the "superior Class of Mankind", offering alienating satire and "Morality in Masquerade" (v). In sum, Longueville tells us, "it may, without the least Arrogance, be affirmed, that [...] this *surprising Narrative* [...]

---

1   For example, the issues of crime, law and personal redemption through the cultivation of land in *The English Hermit* have been discussed in Eve Tavor Bannet, *Transatlantic Stories and the History of Reading, 1720–1810* (Cambridge: Cambridge University Press, 2011), pp. 77–86; the inherently metafictive qualities of the novel have been read by Rivka Swenson in "'Mushrooms, Capers, and Other Sorts of Pickles': Remaking Genre in Peter Longueville's *The Hermit* (1727)", *Rewriting Crusoe: The Robinsonade across Languages, Cultures, and Media*, ed. Jakub Lipski (Lewisburg: Bucknell University Press, 2020), pp. 9–22; its thematic, struc-tural and ideological affinities with the Robinsonade tradition have been surveyed by Artur Blaim in *Robinson Crusoe and His Doubles: The English Robinsonade of the Eighteenth Century* (Frankfurt am Main: Peter Lang, 2016); while the novel's illustration history in the eighteenth century has recently been surveyed by Sandro Jung in "Amplifying Reading Experience: Illus-trations to Longueville's *The English Hermit*, 1727–1799", *English Studies* 103.1 (2022): 42–62.
2   Peter Longueville, *The English Hermit, or the Unparalell'd and Surprizing Adventures of one Philip Quarll* (London: Printed by J. Cluer and A. Campbell for T. Warner in Pater-Noster-Row, and B. Creake at the Bible in Jermyn-Street, St. James's, 1727), p. v. Further references to *The English Hermit* will be parenthetical.

© KONINKLIJKE BRILL NV, LEIDEN, 2024 | DOI:10.1163/9789004692916_004

PETER LONGUEVILLE'S *THE ENGLISH HERMIT* (1727)   33

is certainly of more Use to the publick, than either of them, because every Incident, herein related, is real Matter of Fact" (v). Given that the claim for factuality was nothing more than a perfectly conventional apologetic strategy at the time, it takes a considerable deal of arrogance for a no-name author to openly evaluate his work as superior to the two absolute hits of the 1720s.

That said, Longueville's self-confidence was supported by a formal dexterity that was not derivative, however reliant on Defoe or Swift. Rivka Swenson has argued persuasively for the author's stylistic accomplishments, his poetics of description and his visual imagination,[3] but his competence in contemporary fictional forms and structures is confirmed by a curious, yet creative, narrative packaging of the eponymous hermit's story. Book I, "An Account of how Mr. Quarll was found out, with a Description of his Dress, Habitation, and Utensils; as also, his Conversation with the Persons who first Discovered Him" (1), is a frame narrative centring on the travels and trading affairs of Mr. Dorrington, who features in the Preface as the owner of the "original" manuscript written by the hermit Philip Quarll. Despite the typical Robinsonade motifs indicated in the epigraph summary, this Book gives much more space to Dorrington's various exploits, and reads like a travel narrative. Book II, generically speaking, is a criminal biography: it includes the encountered castaway's life story, which is a series of misdemeanours, however well-meaning and good-natured Quarll seems to be and have been. After the obligatory Newgate scenes, the narrative takes Quarll to the sea rather than the gallows, and sees him marooned on the island where Dorrington finds him in Book I. Finally, Book III is a relatively straightforward Robinsonade narrative, with the exception of its ending: no rescue is needed as Quarll is adamant that he will remain on the island. In this chapter I will argue that the representations of Quarll's body, and its metaphorical and literal transformations, constitute a key to understanding both the novel's strange and surprising structure and its ideological dimensions. I show how the criminal body is saved and redeemed on an Edenic island and how, on the one hand, it follows the rhythm of nature and becomes immersed in the natural environment, and on the other how it internalises the mythical ideal of the New Adam, whose religious and imperial self-discipline helps him conquer the carnal temptations and the wilderness of the land.

The foregrounded role of the body in the novel is already established in the paratextual "threshold of interpretation", to use Gérard Genette's metaphor,[4] in particular the frontispiece (Figure 8) that features castaway Philip Quarll

---

3 Swenson, "Mushrooms, capers, and other sorts of pickles".
4 Gérard Genette, *Paratexts: Thresholds of Interpretation*, trans. J. E. Lewin (Cambridge: Cambridge University Press, 1997).

FIGURE 8 The frontispiece to the first edition of Peter Longueville's *The English Hermit* (1727)
COURTESY OF BEINECKE RARE BOOK AND MANUSCRIPT LIBRARY, YALE UNIVERSITY

PETER LONGUEVILLE'S *THE ENGLISH HERMIT* (1727)   35

depicted with a naked, muscular torso, reminiscent of Renaissance Old Masters' conventions, and the poem "On the Hermit's Solitude", which revolves around the metaphor of resurrection: "From rugged Rocks the Sailor gains a Prize / And Shipwreck'd oft, from Death, to Life arise" (XI).

These two elements of the paratext invite an allegorical reading of the narrative as a story of new life, of a New Adam, characterised by outstanding vitality (we are later informed about him bearing his age "wonderful well" [16]) and what we would now call a naturist way of life (Book III traces his gradual rejection of clothes). Quarll, as depicted in the frontispiece, aligns with Robinsonade representations of imperial masculinity: he is depicted in motion, as if leaving the spot having done his work, his muscles strained, with an axe in hand that symbolises dominance over the natural world, supported by his civilisational achievements in the background and by Monkey Beufidell, an extremely racist variant of Man Friday ("his Monkey, and his Man", as we read in the prefatory poem [xi]). Indeed, as Sandro Jung puts it, he is "a maker depicted in an act" and "the driving force and prime agent" of the island narrative.[5] His patriarchal physiognomy, created by the long beard and a serious expression, fits into Weaver-Hightower's discussion of the God-like, white father figure, evident from *The Tempest*'s Prospero to the nineteenth-century imperial Robinsonade (Marryat's Masterman Ready and Verne's Captain Nemo).[6] But Quarll becomes a father figure out of a criminal; as we read in the prefatory poem, which highlights his transformation from boyhood to adulthood, "He's rais'd a Monarch, from an abject Boy" (xi). Referring to Julia Kristeva, Ian Kinane has written on the conceptualisation of the island as a space of the abject, pointing out that "Islands, as sites of 'custody' and 'banishment', were seen as repositories for the diseased, dysfunctional, antisocial and repressible elements of society – they were abject zones of loss and forgetting, where all unwanted and damaging elements to mainland, continental society were pushed down and sequestered out of sight".[7] The hermit's bodily change, then, his "resurrection" on the island, where he grows from "an abject boy" to a monumental monarch, endows the seemingly loose structure of the novel – and especially the transition from a criminal biography (Book II) to a Robinsonade (Book III) – with an overarching logic, whereby the eliminated, transgressive body redefines itself outside of its original society and starts anew, not exactly re-enacting internalised civilisational patterns, as do Crusoe and other castaway-colonists, but instead finding redemption in a harmonious coexistence with the Edenic abundance surrounding him. Quarll's balance between a proto-ecological immersion in

---

5   Jung, "Amplifying Reading Experience", pp. 45–46.
6   Weaver-Hightower, *Empire Islands*, pp. 67–72.
7   Kinane, *Theorising Literary Islands*, p. 144.

the environment and an imperial ordering of space and use of its resources constitutes the ideological double-voicedness of the narrative that imprints itself on the castaway's body, reconciling – paradoxically – a "primitivist" devolution with imperial growth.

The castaway makes his appearance in Book I in a manner that casts a shadow of ambiguity on his physical shape and identity, and on the island environment. Depending on the poetics of imaginary voyages, the narrative introduces the island as a place out of this world: surrounded by unusual specimens of fish, hardly accessible through the surrounding rocky mountains, and overgrown with a strange type of tree. The preliminary pages, apart from the frontispiece and poem already mentioned, include a sketchy map of the island, which displays a regularity and spatial organisation reminiscent of allegorical representations of imaginary space; in particular, the fountain in the centre brings to mind visual renderings of paradise, typically featuring the Fountain of Life as a transfiguration of Christ in the centre, similar to the famous *Ghent Altarpiece* by the van Eyck brothers (1432). As the visitors, including narrator Edward Dorrington, explore the environs and the castaway's dwelling, his identity as the eponymous "hermit" is purposefully questioned, with Dorrington supposing "that some Hermit did dwell in the Place" (8) and instantly doubting the idea upon seeing arms and an abundance of foods that would be "too Epicurial for an Hermit" (10). In this manner, indications of violence (arms) and carnal pleasure (delicious foods) undermine the castaway's identity as an ascetic hermit, despite the novel's title, and indicate Quarll's susceptibility to earthly weaknesses, which comes to the fore in the criminal biography narrative that follows. When the visitors finally meet the castaway, he is first observed from a distance and considered to be "something like a Man" (12) or "a Giant" (13) (towards the end of the novel he is also labelled "a monstrous English Hermit" [238]), and it takes a closer look for the "formidable Giant" to be recognised as "an ordinary Man" (13) – though one "inspir[ing] Respect":

> the Man [...] appear'd to be a venerable old Man, with a worshipful white Beard, which cover'd his naked Breast; and a long Head of Hair of the same Colour, which, spreading over his Shoulders, hung down to his Loins. (13)

The ensuing conversation between the castaway and Dorrington is body-oriented, with the visitor offering rescue on the grounds of the "Necessaries which [Quarll's] Age requires, as Cloaths to defend the Injuries of the Air, and Meat suitable to the Weakness of [his] Stomach" (15). Doubts concerning his bodily constitution, however, are quickly resolved, as on being asked "did not Age deprive you of Strength", Quarll explains that his life in this "second Garden of *Eden*" is free from earthly longings (16). By highlighting that there is "no forbidden Fruit, nor Women to tempt a Man", he points to what his now rejected life in the "wide World" mostly involved. Bodily discipline, then, allows him to "bear [his] Age wonderful well" (16), which is followed by a demonstration of strength and vigour unusual in a 78-year-old. The recipe for this, as Dorrington is told, is simple: "you must use none but wholesome Exercise, observe a sober Diet, and live a pious Life" (30), and "*Waste not your Vigour [...] on Women, lest Weakness [...] be your Reward*" (31).

With its explicit Biblical references, Book I foregrounds a New Adam whose resurrected body enjoys a prelapsarian union with natural abundance. His continuous labour becomes a happily accepted form of discipline that facilitates a remarkable bodily change. His physical evolution depends on an acceptance of "island infection", which is presented here as a "primitivist" way of life contrasted with the corruption and never-ending hassle of "civilised" living, including sexual relationships with women, considered not only as temptresses who precipitate man's fall but also as quasi-vampiric enemies depriving men of bodily health. Quarll's vigour, then, is a fantasy of discipline and celibacy, and an allegory of masculine sufficiency[8] that sees the female body as a threat. In this, *The English Hermit* elaborates on *Robinson Crusoe's* asexuality (in the first volume), which may be read as imperial and economic sublimation, but offers a more complex treatment of bodily discipline in the context of Quarll's "rake's progress" in the narrative of his pre-island life.

The account of Quarll's fall in Book II opens with scenes of childhood, showing the would-be castaway as an "extraordinary neat and clean" child, who "was naturally very handsome, being tall for his Age, and well shap'd, his Features regular and proportion'd, his Complexion fair, his Hair long and curling, his Countenance mild and sprightly" (70). Physical beauty, as was typical of early eighteenth-century fiction, by extension connotes innocence and nobility, thus implying that the story of moral degeneration to follow will partly absolve Quarll of his transgression. The suggestion is that this fall, like Adam's, was precipitated by others: first a thief and a drunkard, who in the narrative is purposely dubbed as "Seducer" (74) and "Serpent" (75), and then a "Drury-Lane Nymph" with "Basilick's Eyes" (79–80), who quickly tricks him into matrimony, thereby inaugurating a series of morally dubious relationships with women. All in all, polygamous Quarll marries four times, and even if the narrative voice

---

8 See Weaver-Hightower, *Empire Islands*, pp. 77–80.

goes some way towards minimising his own agency and placing him in the role of victim, no discursive stratagem can justify his behaviour towards the second wife, whom he imprisons in the countryside on the grounds of her alleged mental instability. The biographical narrative presents him as a victim to the ruinous, even satanic schemes of the women he encounters in his life – "every one equal Plagues" (134) – but, in fact, Quarll is little more than a rakish predator. His progress is imprinted on his dressed body, very much like Hogarth's Tom Rakewell, whose first decision on having inherited his father's fortune was to obtain for himself a new set of garments (*A Rake's Progress*, 1732–34, Plate 1). Quarll's social mobility is marked by subsequent changes of clothes that correspond to his new roles – from sailor (78–79), to guard (86–88), to tradesman (136) – and the final transformation is to that of a London beau: "very handsomely dress'd, and his Behaviour much better polish'd than formerly" (151). A typical narrative of rise and fall, his life story finds its conclusion in Newgate, when the polygamist is due to be sentenced to death at Tyburn.

The body in Book II is thus constructed – implicitly, between the lines of the quasi-hagiographic narrative – as the criminal, transgressive body that succumbs to illicit pleasures (polygamy), uncritically welcomes society's obsession with artifice and masquerade (fashionable clothes), and is eventually made to face just punishment. In a typical criminal biography, the conventional conclusion of this kind of narrative would be a detailed Tyburn scene with the criminal body exposed and punished, much as with Defoe's *Account of Jonathan Wild* (1725), at the end of which we read about the Tyburn mob ready to "tear [Wild] to pieces".[9] In fact, this is what the second (imprisoned) wife wishes on Quarll when she vows that she will *"tear that Villain to pieces"* (110). The "tearing to pieces" also connotes the potential, and often typical aftermath of a Tyburn execution: public anatomical dissection. Since the sixteenth century, executions provided a significant means of satisfying a growing demand for corpses for anatomical research; indeed, before the Anatomy Act of 1832, they were the only legitimate source of dead bodies.[10] This public "tearing to pieces" is memorably depicted by Hogarth, whose visual criminal biography, *The Four Stages of Cruelty* (1751), closes with the scene of the public dissection of the executed Tom Nero (Plate 4: *The Reward of Cruelty*). The inscription at the base

---

9   Daniel Defoe, *The True and Genuine Account of the Life and Actions of the Late Jonathan Wild*, *Jonathan Wild*, by Henry Fielding, ed. David Nokes (London: Penguin Books, 1986), p. 257.

10   Andrew T. Chamberlain, "Morbid Osteology: Evidence for Autopsies, Dissection and Surgical Training from the Newcastle Infirmary Burial Ground (1753–1845)", *Anatomical Dissection in Enlightenment England and Beyond: Autopsy, Pathology and Display*, ed. Piers Mitchell (Farnham: Ashgate, 2012), p. 11.

PETER LONGUEVILLE'S *THE ENGLISH HERMIT* (1727)   39

of the image offers a macabre contemplation on the final stage of punishment exercised on the dead body:

> Behold the Villain's dire disgrace!
> Not Death itself can end.
> He finds no peaceful Burial-Place,
> His breathless Corse, no friend.
> Torn from the Root, that wicked Tongue,
> Which daily swore and curst!
> Those Eyeballs from their Sockets wrung,
> That glow'd with lawless Lust!
> His Heart expos'd to prying Eyes,
> To Pity has no claim;
> But, dreadful! from his Bones shall rise,
> His Monument of Shame.[11]

Alluding to the Biblical prophecy of man's resurrection, the poem underlines the religious implications of "tearing to pieces", suggesting that the punishment compromises the promise of redemption, thus doubling the price the criminal must pay. It also foregrounds the crime of illicit desire, "lawless Lust", partly thematised in Plate 3 (*Cruelty in Perfection*), making it a meaningful context for Quarll's story.

The sentenced polygamist in Book II should expect little more than the fate described and depicted in contemporary criminal biographies, but thanks to a royal pardon secured by his well-wishing acquaintances (on condition that he leaves the country), Quarll only suffers a metaphorical death at sea when he is shipwrecked and marooned on a desert island, functioning as a penal colony of sorts. His resurrection from this metaphorical death, however, is preceded by bodily pain – a beating exercised by the watery element against Quarll's "worthless Carcass" (156), as he describes it. Spending the first night on the island cliff, he was "continually beaten with the dashing back of the Sea, was both bruis'd and num'd" (154). Since up to this point Book II has paid considerable attention to Quarll's susceptibility to the allure of artifice and masquerade, the fact that after this beating he pulls off his clothes to dry them (154) can be interpreted as a symbolic distancing from his former life, with his nakedness, already allegorised in Book I, suggesting a new birth from the waters of the sea. While the personalised "Fury of the Sea" in the shipwreck scene in *Crusoe* was meant as an indicator of the castaway's helplessness and passivity, the beating

---

11   William Hogarth, "The Reward of Cruelty", https://www.royalacademy.org.uk/art-artists /work-of-art/the-reward-of-cruelty-i-four-stages-of-cruelty-i-plate-4.

exercised by the sea in *The English Hermit* is further allegorised as punishment when the exhausted castaway is tormented by a nightmare:

> He dream'd he was in a terrible Tempest, and the Ship he was in dash'd backwards and forwards thro' the Waves with prodigious Violence, the Clouds pouring down vast Streams of liquid Fire, and the raging Ocean all in Flame, in this dismal Condition he knew not what to do, but spying some Land as he thought, at a little distance from the Ship, he was endeavouring to get there, but not daring to venture the Sea, which he imagin'd was like a Caldron of Oil in a Blaze, resolv'd to try whether he could not jump ashore; but just as he was going to leap, he saw a horrid frightful Monster, with glaring Eyes and open Mouth, rush from the boiling Flames, and make at him, to devour him, which scar'd him out of his Sleep. (155)

Quarll dreams of the sea as a hellish space ready to devour him. The typical imagery of perpetual punishment in the afterlife, involving flames, cauldrons and monsters, is brought in to sustain the counterfactual narrative of the criminal's death and eternal damnation that, in the actual narrative, transforms into a story of redemption. The beating of the sea is thus also a quasi-baptism that gives the castaway a new life. The same symbolic pattern is repeated once Quarll passes over the rocky cliffs and enters the island by wading naked through a lake.

Quarll's transformation from a womaniser to a hermit seeking unity with the environment is established in a way that recognises parallels between sexual pleasure and love of natural abundance – parallels that would later be explored in Tournier's *Friday* in the (in)famous scene of love-making with earth. In *The English Hermit*, the praise of natural scenery and sensuous descriptions of food in Book I receive an allegorical framing at the beginning of Book III, when Quarll, who is continuously tormented by dreams, has a vision that is prompted by overindulgence in seafood, with obvious sexual connotations:

> his Rest was very much disturb'd with the frightful Dream of being attack'd by a terrible Monster, such as never was heard of either for Bigness or Grimness, which pursu'd him, till having run himself out of Breath, he was forc'd to lie expos'd to his Fury; but was prevented being devour'd by a grave old Gentlewoman of a most graceful and majestick Countenance, at whose sudden Appearance the Monster fled. (161)

As we know, it is not the first time Quarll has been tormented by monsters in his dreams, but this one also stages the figure of a redeemer. Quarll wishes to

PETER LONGUEVILLE'S *THE ENGLISH HERMIT* (1727) 41

pay her his respects but learns that she is everywhere, always ready to stand with the helpless. The hermit interprets the dream as God's Providence saving him from Death, but there are also echoes of the figure of omnipresent Mother Nature in the figure of the old woman. If this vision establishes the New Paradise as a space of redemption from death, the follow-up dream, prompted by Quarll's worries about "the Dread of those Hardships he must probably undergo" (163), centres on the abundance of the Edenic space, alleviating the fear of hardships, such as cold, with clearly erotic implications:

> [H]e saw an old Man resembling Time [...] with Heaps of Snow and Hail about him, and himself very busy with making more; at his side stood a very beautiful Woman, whose Shape and Make was uncommon, and her Features and Complexion extraordinary; but what surpriz'd him most, was her having three pairs of Breasts, wonderfully handsome, and curiously plac'd, which seem'd to adorn her Bosom far more than the richest Stomager made of Diamonds and Pearls could do; so that which in other Women would look monstrous, was in her an Addition to her matchless Beauty.
>
> The Sight of that most perfect and compleat Woman, warm'd his Blood, which the Coldness of the Place had chill'd, and tempted him to come nearer the Charmer; as he advanc'd, every Step he made, seem'd to add Strength to his Limbs, and Vigour to his Life, which made him desirous to come nearer to the Person from whom he receiv'd such beneficial Effluvias, but was suddenly stop'd by the old Man's turning towards him with a grim and surly Countenance, which threatened his nearer Approach with Evil. (163–164)

The figure of the "old Man resembling Time" – the description of whom resonates with the iconography of winter, as if to respond to Quarll's fears for bodily hardship and, by extension, growing old and dying – is juxtaposed with the beautiful woman, interpreted by Quarll as Nature (165), whose three pairs of breasts symbolise natural abundance. She brings warmth to the dreaming observer and increases his bodily vigour. The hermit's as it were gigantic qualities, as presented in Book I, are thus contextualised within an allegorical frame that reveals how he has reoriented his quest for bodily pleasure: from quasi-vampiric (in his view) women of the metropolis to feminised and sexualised natural abundance.

Quarll's unity with the island, then, is for the most part established through his use of natural resources, especially food, but initially without the colonial control over this space. This is most readily visible in his gradual shift from feeding on fish to feeding on roots: "my Fish is almost gone, and not certain of more, I must by Degrees bring my self to live upon Roots, which I hope will never be wanting, being the natural Product of this Island" (172). Noticing that roots constitute the main source of sustenance for the monkeys inhabiting the island, Quarll does not engage in any violent struggle with them, although he realises that he could easily "kill several" and "disperse the rest" (172). Instead, he peacefully helps himself to the roots, and when he later comes for more, with his clothes now removed due to the heat, he realises that, as the New Adam, he inspires awe in these creatures and is welcomed by them as a "natural" inhabitant of the island:

> This surprizing Reverence from those Creatures, set him upon deep Reflections on what could be the Cause thereof; whether it might not proceed from the Proximity of their Shape and his; but then said he, my Stature and Colour of Skin is so different from theirs, that they cannot but distinguish I am not of their kind: No, it must be a Remnant of that Awe, intail'd by Nature upon all Animals, to that most noble and compleat Masterpiece of the Creation call'd *Man*, which now appearing in the State he was first created in, and undisguis'd by Cloaths, renews a Smatch of that Respect he has forfeited by his fatal Transgression, which ever since oblig'd him to hide the Beauty of his Fabrick under a gaudy Disguise, which often renders him ridiculous to the rest of Mankind, and generally obnoxious to all other Creatures, making a Pride of what he ought to be asham'd of: Well, adds he, since it was my Cloaths as bred the Antipathy, I will remove that Cause, which will suit both the Nature of those Animals, and my own Circumstances; so from that time he resolves to go naked, till the Hardness of the Weather oblig'd him to put something on. (174)

Given Quarll's immersion in the world of artifice and masquerade, as related in Book II, the positive evaluation of his "going native" narrated above depends on a pattern of quasi-ritualistic unmasking, revealing the true nature beneath the disguises of civilisation. The hermit takes a step back, revoking cultural refinement, in order to – paradoxically – vindicate himself as "that most noble and compleat Masterpiece of the Creation call'd *Man*". When he later discovers clothes in a chest that the sea brought to the island from the wreck of his ship, Quarll corrects Crusoe's hesitation over seemingly useless money, and declares: "these [...] neither the Owner, nor I, do want" (183).

Tellingly, the hermit's "primitivist" transformation happens upon the castaway's encountering "Others", or the island's inhabitants – the monkeys, who now accept him as a local. Their "awe" and "respect" situates this story of change in a mythical context, albeit without the typical indications of the New

Adam's spatial control and conquest. This is made clear in the ensuing walk around the island, which lacks – not accidentally, I would argue – the conventional monarch-of-all-I-survey scene featuring the castaway climbing a hill. Rather than establishing his dominance vertically, Quarll moves horizontally, without following a preconceived pattern, and marvels at the beauties of the island environment. As he observes the rocky hills encircling the island, he recognises the shapes of various architectural forms, from the Tower of Babel to urban houses, which allude to the poetics of atemporality belonging to *voyages imaginaires*; or, as Foucault suggests with reference to heterotopias, a quality that gives one "a sort of absolute break with their traditional time" by "constituting a place of all times that is itself outside of time".[12] Thus tinged with the element of the supernatural, the island exists, as it were, out of time – as a heterotopic space – while simultaneously conceptualising the circularity of change that contrasts the imperial narrative of linear progress. As the hermit engages with the environment, starting a conversation with the hills that echo his voice and noting the vestiges of abandoned civilisation, he reaches the fountain at the centre of the island: the source of life. His exploration of the land, then, is constituted not by a panoramic view from on high, such as characterises imperialist Robinsonades, but by observing, and indeed marvelling at, the land from the inside, and being immersed in it.

In contrast to Crusoe, who is largely insensitive to the beauties of the environment, Quarll repeatedly walks around the island to contemplate its views and to derive sensual pleasure, which is reported in a style that is appropriately poetic in its alliterative and onomatopoeic qualities:

> So he walks up the Land, which he found very level, cover'd with a delightful green Grass, and adorn'd with Trees of divers Sorts, Shapes, and Height, inhabited with several sorts of curious singing Birds, of various Colours and Notes, which entertain'd him with their melodious Harmony during his Walk. (179)

Such delicious pleasures for the eyes and ears are complemented with others that satiate the hermit's nose and palate; the New Adam's immersion in natural abundance thus corrects his criminal sensuality in the pre-island narrative. Quarll remains a man of pleasure, but the story of his new life on the island dramatises a change – from his susceptibility to illicit desire to non-sexual sensualism.

---

12   Foucault, "Of Other Spaces", p. 26.

That Quarll is now one with the environment is made clear when the change of seasons, from winter to spring, is imprinted on the hermit's body. The mythical dimension of the cycle of nature is explicitly established in the text in a conventionally poetic transition, personifying the seasons and their associated winds: "Boreas [...], grown faint with hard blowing, is forc'd to retreat into his Cave; gentle Zephirus [...] now comes forth to usher in the blooming Spring" (188). Just as the island's vegetation is revived, so is the hermit, now living in perfect harmony with the environment, not only in terms of how it sustains him with its fruits, but also how its rhythm of change translates itself into Quarll's biological constitution:

> *Quarll* also, whom bad Weather had confin'd within Doors a considerabe Time, which had in a great Measure numb'd his Limbs, and dull'd his Sense, now finds himself quite reviv'd, he no longer can keep within, the fair Weather invites him out, the singing Birds on every Side call to him, Nature it self fetches him out to behold her Treasures. (189)

Such indications of the hermit's revival are repeated later in the narrative, thus reinforcing the circularity of the natural order with an inherent textual circularity at the formal level. However, when Quarll appears at the peak of his "primitivist" transition, the novel's language of the body moves from proto-ecological to imperial discourse, from representations of the sensual body immersed in the environment to the body politic.

This change is signalled by two scenes that combine political allegory with the castaway's own reinterpretation of his role as New Adam. The first involves Quarll going to the seashore in search of oysters:

> he creeps to the North-east Side of the Rock, at the Foot of which lay, an extraordinary large Whale, which the late high Wind had cast there, and dy'd for want of Water. [...] there were Shoals of small Fishes swimming about it in the shallow Water wherein it lay, as rejoicing at its Death; thus said he, the oppress'd rejoice at a Tyrant's Fall; what Number of these have been destroy'd to make this monstrous bulk of Fat; well, happy are they, who, like me, are under Heaven's Government only; so with his Knife, which he always carried in his Pocket, cuts several Slices of the Whale, and throws them to the small Fishes, saying, 'tis but just ye should at last feed on that which so long fed on you. (190)

Alluding to Thomas Hobbes's defence of absolutism and the allegory of the Biblical Leviathan as an embodiment of the state, this scene coheres with *The*

English Hermit's later political visions, which elevate Georgian rule, such as Quarll's imagining in (novelistic) 1713 a great king who accedes to the throne (George I took the crown in 1714). At the same time, the hermit's thoughts about the whale and cutting of its flesh to feed the fish impose the circular order of nature onto the degenerated body politic, now serving as food to those it exploited. Since the scene immediately precedes Quarll's decision to feed on animals (other than seafood) and interfere more profoundly in the life of the island – following his reflections on his role as New Adam in the Garden of Eden and the divine permission to subjugate the earth (192) – it is also a sign for the evolving colonist that warns him against becoming, like Crusoe, an absolutist "King of the Island". In sustaining his body through the exploitation of animals on the island, Quarll parallels the predator-prey relationship that he recognised in the whale and the fish, while the scene's political allegory is doubled by Quarll's manner of hunting: he catches hare-like animals by the neck with what he labels "killing Noozes" (192). In administering to the "hares" the punishment he himself eventually evaded, Quarll embodies the power of the state, and his troubled conscience – on seeing that one of the "hares" was big with little ones, he "grieved" and "repented" (192) – may well be visualising the dead whale to him, "this monstrous bulk of Fat". And indeed, Quarll soon realises that not much separates a predator from its prey when he becomes a victim of pirate raids on "his" island and is on the verge of being bound with rope and kidnapped in order to be displayed as a Gulliverian curiosity in the wider world.

Nevertheless, Quarll does transform into a colonist, and the hunting scenes are followed by his decision to expand his settlement. He finally calls himself "Lord of this Island" and reflects on the threat of "his" island attracting the attention of some Princes who may "claim a Right to it" and appoint "extorting Governors" (209). Quarll's colony, then, is thought of as a heterotopic space separated from the global imperialist network, delineated by Dorrington's travels in the frame narrative of Book I, especially as he continues to visual-ise political conflicts in the wider world. Quarll sees himself as providentially freed from late-seventeenth-century political turmoil (the time frame of the narrative), and, as he observes sectarian divisions among the monkeys inhab-iting the island and their battles over food, he readily assumes the role of peacemaker. The hermit becomes the rational head of the body politic, the source of law and order, and after his first successful interventions the mon-keys directly invite him to intervene when another battle is about to take place, and one of their number, named Beufidell by the hermit, voluntarily becomes his servant. The connection established between Monkey Beufidell and Cru-soe's Friday, as well as the hermit's continual parallels between the animal and the human world, suggest an allegorical reading of Quarll's dealing with the monkeys whereby the animals function as racist embodiments of the colonial other, inviting and expecting the Western castaway's involvement so that law and order can be enforced. Echoing Gulliver's activities on the land of the Lilliput and Friday's famous "they willing love learn", which encourages Crusoe to intervene in the cannibal society,[13] and foreshadowing a number of similar episodes in the later Robinsonades (such as *Peter Wilkins*, *William Bingfield* or *Crusoe Richard Davis*), the scene is a conventional allegory of the imperial rule established with the permission and to the "advantage" of the subjugated others.

Quarll's evolution into a fully fledged colonist culminates in his reflections on the issues of inheritance and legacy, which conceptually juxtapose the evanescence of the hermit's biological body, as part of the circular order of nature, with the expected linear continuation of the body politic. Consequently, accepting that Providence may strand another castaway on the island at a future point and bestow the property upon him, "he draws a Map of the whole Estate, and made an Inventory of every dividual Tenement, Appurtenances, Messuages, Goods and Chattels, as also a Draught of the Terms and Conditions he is to hold the here-mention'd Possessions upon" (211–212). The "Terms and Conditions" regulate the religious life as well as the discipline of repetitive labour so as to "keep every Thing in the same Order and Cleanness he shall find them in" (213). In this, the hermit re-enacts Crusoe's tendency for cataloguing and ordering, which, as Wolfram Schmidgen points out, establishes "an indisputable sense of connection" between the castaway and his surroundings, and "registers a radical anxiety over the possibility of turning the island into property".[14]

In the end, however, just as the "primitivist" body was not consistent in its proto-ecological evolution, so the self-disciplined imperial body – the head of the heterotopic body politic – is compromised towards the end of the narrative: first when Quarll is ready to let himself be rescued and taken back to the world he openly despised, and later, when he longs for a female companion, as if he had not had enough of (in his view) exploitative women. On both occasions, his body is a slave to passions which, as Hobbes put it, "are not called voluntary; for they proceed not from, but are the will, and the will is not voluntary".[15] In *Robinson Crusoe*, the chief passion that is the protagonist's "will" is his unsatiated desire for movement and change, which forces him to

---

13   Defoe, *Robinson Crusoe*, p. 188.
14   Schmidgen, *Eighteenth-Century Fiction and the Law of Property*, p. 38.
15   Thomas Hobbes, *The Elements of Law: Natural and Politic*, ed. Ferdinand Tönnies (Cambridge: Cambridge University Press, 1928), p. 48.

leave whatever stability he might temporarily enjoy. Echoes of this can be seen in *The English Hermit*: even if Book I shows Quarll as not willing to abandon the stability of his solitary life on the island, Book III reveals that the shadowy presence behind the carefully delineated ideals of the "primitivist" body immersed in the environment and of the self-disciplined imperial body is a dynamic psycho-somatic construct that can easily throw either of the two off-balance, psycho-somatic in as much as the passions reveal themselves through the body's uncontrollable actions and movements. This can be best seen when the hermit is expecting rescue (which does not eventually take place): "his Heart alters its Motion, his Blood stops from its common Course, his Sinews are all stagnated, which entirely unframes his Reason, and makes him a Stranger to his own Inclination" (215–216). The frames of the two bodily constructs are thus "unframed", as the body is endowed with an agency that is paradoxically autonomous and independent of reason. The drama of Quarll's passions alludes to how Defoe rendered his own hermit figure in *The Farther Adventures of Robinson Crusoe* – that of the mysterious Russian prince, who accepted his banishment to Siberia and renounced civilisation. The prince argues very well in support of his detached life, but when Crusoe offers to save him, his will is destabilised: "I could see in his very Face, that what I said put his Spirits into an exceeding Ferment; his Colour frequently chang'd, his Eyes look'd red, and his Heart flutter'd, that it might be even perceiv'd in his Countenance [...]".[16]

Quarll's body, then, is a deeply metafictional construct: apart from embodying the double-voiced discourse of the novel that confronts the Robinsonade's conventional imperial programming with potentially radical, proto-ecological messages, it captures the genre's central preoccupation with, as it were, compulsive mobility. As a discursive space, the body in *The English Hermit* combines conflicting perspectives: it foregrounds a "primitivist" devolution as a road to both prelapsarian unity with nature and colonial ventures orchestrated by a muscular imperialist, very much reminiscent of Wyeth's and Fairbanks's renditions of Crusoe; and through staging a clash of Crusoesque self-discipline with a passions-driven instability of the body, it ponders more general questions about the castaway's need for change and movement. Longueville clearly corrects Defoe in his treatment of the castaway's body, most ostensibly by rewriting Crusoe's obsession with clothes, but *The English Hermit* is also deeply invested, through its discreet points of convergence with the ur-text, in wider concerns about the passion for change that lies at the core of *Robinson Crusoe* and the Robinsonade tradition in general.

---

16   Daniel Defoe, *The Farther Adventures of Robinson Crusoe*, ed. Maximillian E. Novak, Irving N. Rothman and Manuel Schonhorn (Lewisburg: Bucknell University Press, 2022), p. 249.

CHAPTER 3

Robert Paltock's *Peter Wilkins* (1751): Mythical Androgyny and Evolutionary Hybridisation

Dubbed "the illegitimate offspring of no very natural conjunction betwixt *Gulliver*'s Travels and *Robinson Crusoe*",[1] Robert Paltock's *The Life and Adventures of Peter Wilkins, a Cornish Man* (1751) was received sceptically in its time, though it was translated relatively promptly into French and German.[2] Several decades needed to pass for it to became a "cult book" in Romanticism; its reputation in the period 1780–1860 was established by "over forty editions, reprints or versions, including adaptations for pantomime".[3] It was praised by such figures as S. T. Coleridge and Mary Shelley,[4] and was believed to have been ahead of its time:

> Considered as a work of imagination, it appeared at a season, either too late or too early, to captivate the fancies or strike deep root in the minds of men. At that particular period [...] the imagination, lying as it were torpid, awaited the moment when it should be again called into life and action [...].[5]

And, indeed, the novel's readers needed a very vivid imagination to process Wilkins's strange and surprising adventures, recounted in a manner that combines the narrative traditions of Tobias Smollett (the pre-island episodes), Daniel Defoe (the Robinsonade section) and Jonathan Swift

---

1 *Monthly Review* 4 (1750): 157.

2 This chapter uses some of the material included in my other two publications on *Peter Wilkins*: Jakub Lipski, "Robert Paltock, *The Life and Adventures of Peter Wilkins* (1751)", *Handbook of the British Novel in the Long Eighteenth Century*, ed. Katrin Berndt and Alessa Johns (Berlin and Boston: De Gruyter, 2022), pp. 243–258; Jakub Lipski, "Three Mid-Eighteenth-Century Mashups: Hybridity and Conflicted Discourse in Robert Paltock's *Peter Wilkins* and Its Early Imitations", *1650–1850: Ideas, Aesthetics, and Inquiries in the Early Modern Era*, Vol. 28 (Lewisburg: Bucknell University Press, 2023), pp. 119–139.

3 Nora Crook, "*Peter Wilkins*: A Romantic Cult Book", *Reviewing Romanticism*, ed. Philip W. Martin and Robin Jarvis (London: Macmillan, 1992), p. 86.

4 Crook, "*Peter Wilkins*: A Romantic Cult Book", pp. 86–98.

5 *Retrospective Review*, VII (1823), i. 122–4; quoted after Christopher Bentley. "Introduction", *The Life and Adventures of Peter Wilkins*, by Robert Paltock, ed. Christopher Bentley (London: Oxford University Press, 1973), p. XIII.

© KONINKLIJKE BRILL NV, LEIDEN, 2024 | DOI:10.1163/9789004692916_005

(the confrontation with other societies). The story sees Peter Wilkins shipwrecked on an unwelcoming rock near the South Pole, after a series of Bildungsroman-like misadventures and highly turbulent seafaring. From the rock, an underground cataract takes him to Graundevolet, a twilight island surrounded by rocky mountains (similar to those in Longueville's *The English Hermit*). In the climax of the survival section Wilkins rescues Youwarkee, who literally falls from the sky. She is a Gawrey, a winged woman,[6] and proves a perfect wife who gives him numerous offspring. The family-life section focusing on Peter's relationship with Youwarkee and completing the narrative of island survival subsequently evolves into the colonial section, a Swiftian public-engagement narrative, though deprived of *Gulliver's Travels'* satire, which sees Wilkins travelling to his wife's homeland. He helps defeat this country's enemies and reforms the land according to the ideals of Western "Enlightenment". The "strangeness" of the novel in general would likely have appealed to Romantic-era tastes, as would the narrative of Wilkins and Youwarkee's developing relationship, involving sensuous descriptions of the body and their androgynous union.

After falling into prolonged critical oblivion in the mid-nineteenth century, and remaining there throughout much of the twentieth, *Peter Wilkins* has gradually been rediscovered by criticism. The novel has been discussed in genre-oriented studies, illustrating such textual traditions as the imaginary voyage, utopia, science fiction and, of course, the Robinsonade.[7] Jason Pearl has read *Peter Wilkins* in the broader context of eighteenth-century fiction, showing how the text complicates some of the binaries constructing the myth of the "rise of the novel", such as the "bias for realism" and the foregrounding of

---

6 The theme of flying in the novel might explain the choice of the protagonist's name. As James Sambrook suggests, it is possibly an allusion to John Wilkins (1614–1672), who wrote in *Mathematical Magic* that man might at some point learn to fly. James Sambrook, "Paltock, Robert", *Oxford Dictionary of National Biography*, https://www.oxforddnb.com/ (Oxford: Oxford University Press, 2004).

7 See, for example, Philip Babcock Gove, *The Imaginary Voyage in Prose Fiction: A History of Its Criticism and a Guide for Its Study* (New York: Columbia University Press, 1941), pp. 320–327; Paul Baines, "'Able Mechanick': *The Life and Adventures of Peter Wilkins* and the Eighteenth-Century Fantastic Voyage", *Anticipations: Essays on Early Science Fiction and Its Precursors*, ed. David Seed (Syracuse: Syracuse University Press, 1995), pp. 1–25; David Fausett, *Images of the Antipodes in the Eighteenth Century: A Study in Stereotyping* (Amsterdam and Atlanta: Rodopi, 1995), pp. 72–85; Alessa Johns, *Women's Utopias of the Eighteenth Century* (Urbana and Chicago: University of Illinois Press, 2003), pp. 11–12; and Christine Rees, *Utopian Imagination and Eighteenth-Century Fiction* (London and New York: Routledge, 1996), pp. 73–122.

50   CHAPTER 3

Western experience.[8] Socio-culturally oriented perspectives, in turn, have prioritised Paltock's rather non-standard approach to such issues as race, slavery and gender.[9]

This chapter adds to this growing body of criticism by elaborating on issues that, even if present in the critical debate, have not yet been fully accounted for: Wilkins's androgynous relationship with the winged woman Youwarkee, the implicit fantasy of bodily transformation and the resulting evolutionary hybridisation, both metaphorical (represented by Wilkins's flying machine) and real (embodied by Wilkins and Youwarkee's offspring). I will first show how the myth of the Androgyne is reworked to construct a narrative of the utopian family Robinsonade, with Wilkins and Youwarkee communicating naturally, sharing duties, exploring the potential of their different bodily constitutions and finally giving life to hybrid offspring, metonymically representing a different kind of Robinsonade narrative: one in which the encounter with the other gives way to evolutionary change through hybridisation. I will also show how this progressive message is compromised throughout the narrative, and especially in the final section of the novel, where there is little mention of Wilkins's hybrid family; emphasis is instead placed on his utopian revolutions in Youwarkee's homeland, which, however well meaning, become yet another realisation of a colonial fantasy.

The centrality of the body to *Peter Wilkins* is already established on the title page, which informs readers that the novel is "Illustrated with several CUTS, clearly and distinctly representing the Structure and Mechanism of the Wings of the Glums [the males of the flying humanoids] and Gawrys, and the Manner in which they use them either to swim or fly" (1).[10] The prints (Figures 9 and 10) were created by Louis-Philippe Boitard (fl. 1733–1767), who was a relatively successful London-based engraver of French origin, and the son of better-known François Boitard, of Jacob Tonson's circle.[11] Importantly,

---

8   Jason H. Pearl, "*Peter Wilkins* and the Eighteenth-Century Novel", SEL *Studies in English Literature 1500–1900* 57.3 (2017): 541.

9   See, for example, Peter Merchant, "Robert Paltock and the Refashioning of 'Inkle and Yarico'", *Eighteenth-Century Fiction* 9.1 (1996): 37–50; and Elizabeth Hagglund and Jonathan Laidlow, "'A Man might find every thing in your Country': Improvement, Patriarchy, and Gender in Robert Paltock's *The Life and Adventures of Peter Wilkins*", *Gender and Utopia in the Eighteenth Century: Essays in English and French Utopian Writing*, ed. Nicole Pohl and Brenda Tooley (Burlington: Ashgate, 2007), pp. 133–146.

10   References to *Peter Wilkins* will be parenthetical and will use the 1973 Oxford edition.

11   On granting the copyright of his novel to Jacob Robinson and Robert Dodsley in 1749, Paltock secured not only a modest sum of 21 pounds but also a set of Boitard's engravings. Sambrook, "Paltock, Robert".

FIGURE 9   Louis-Philippe Boitard, *A Gawrey Extended for Flight*, an illustration to Robert Paltock's *Peter Wilkins* (1751)
THE PUBLIC DOMAIN REVIEW

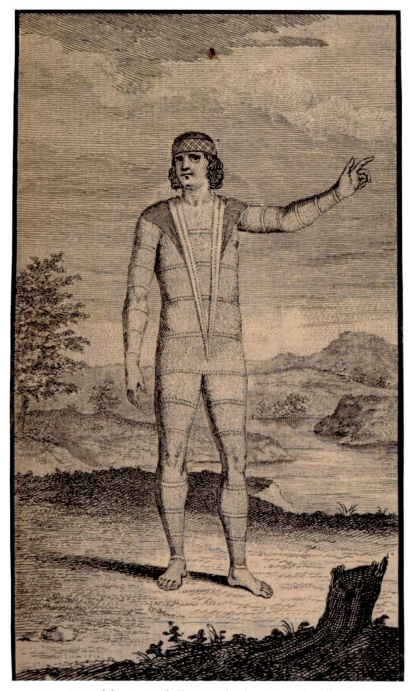

FIGURE 10   Louis-Philippe Boitard, *The Front of a Glumm Dressed*, an illustration to Robert Paltock's *Peter Wilkins* (1751)
THE PUBLIC DOMAIN REVIEW

ROBERT PALTOCK'S *PETER WILKINS* (1751)   53

these illustrations were not a later embellishment, but a textualised element integrated within the first edition of the novel not only by the publisher via the title page, but also by the novelist, who refers to the images in the course of the narrative. The visual elements do indeed focus on the machinery of the "graundee", that is, the wings that can also form a natural boat to be used on the water, but at the same time reveal much of what is beneath, following a classical iconography of bodily beauty. As such, they correspond to the descriptive poetics in the novel that combines sensuality with nuanced representations of the graundee and its mechanics.

Boitard's illustrations also succeed in conveying the novel's ideological double voice, whereby the take on otherness oscillates between recognition and appropriation, respect and colonial subjugation. The theatrical postures of the Glumm and Gawrey, on the one hand, make them pose as exhibits in a cabinet of curiosities; on the other, through the presence of classical iconography previously mentioned, they render an inherent nobility belonging to the "others", thus emphasising and responding to Wilkins's remarks on Youwarkee's "incomparable Shape" and "excellent Form" (108). "The Front of a Glumm Dresst" (Figure 8), meanwhile, is indicative of power and mastery; it is modelled on the genre of the travel portrait, with the Glumm depicted against the welcoming background of the island.

The source of the double voice, I would argue, lies in the novel's complex generic constitution. Alongside reconciling the various traditions of eighteenth-century prose fiction, *Peter Wilkins* also wavers between two castaway narrative variants: the story of a paradise regained and colonial progress, respectively, in a way repeating *The English Hermit*'s juxtaposition of natural circularity with imperial linearity. The novel's engagement with the myth of the Androgyne reflects the Edenic narrative line, with Wilkins and Youwarkee presented as perfect lovers re-enacting the myth of origin and, through their union, engendering a new beginning. This perspective is suggested when towards the end of the narrative Wilkins learns about the national mythology of Doorpt Swangeantine, Youwarkee's homeland:

> this State, by the Tradition of our Ragams [i.e. priests], has subsisted eleven thousand Years; for before that time, the great Mountain *Emina* [...] roaring and raging in its own Bowels for many Ages; at last burst asunder with great Violence, and threw up numberless unformed fleshy Masses to the very Stars; two of which, happening in their Passage to touch the Side of the black Mountain [in Doorpt Swangeantine], for all the rest fell into the Sea and were lost, lodged there, and lying close together as they grew, united to each other, till they were joined in one;

and in process of time, by the Dews of Heaven, became a Glumm and a Gawrey; but being so linked together by the Adhesion of their Flesh, they were obliged both to move which way either would; living thus a long time in great Love and Fondness for each other. (321–322)

The myth goes on to recount how they had children, then separated when they were no longer in perfect concord, and finally reunited, being old and unable to live without each other. More importantly, in the context of Wilkins's decision to settle in this country with his family and his plans to build a new city following Western ideas of harmony and order,[12] the story instils the implication that castaway Wilkins – who was not lost at sea like his companions, or like most of the "fleshy Masses" in the narrative presented above – and Youwarkee (who was a castaway, too, having crashed onto Wilkins's island from the sky), re-enact the story of national origin, this time through a fantasy of positively valued miscegenation. The novelistic rewrite of mythical androgyny as an embodiment of a complete union of the bodies takes up much of Volume I's island section and involves sensuality and eroticism, a harmonious division of labour, and a fantasy of hybridisation.

The novel's sensual descriptions and erotic scenes, in a manner reminiscent of *The English Hermit* (albeit here, unlike in Longueville's novel, the fantasies become part of the island experience), are framed by fairly straightforward indications of the castaway's polygamic disposition, thus adding to what Daniel Cook calls the "sexed up" variant of the Robinsonade, and compensating for the strange and surprising lack of such content in *Robinson Crusoe*.[13] A canonical example in this tradition was Henry Neville's *The Isle of Pines* (1668), a proto-Robinsonade featuring George Pine cast away with four women, and whose main preoccupation was populating the island and then coupling his numerous offspring with one another. The allure of the island as a space where one is legitimised to transgress conventional social norms, as a space "linked to illicit sexual desire",[14] has remained topical ever since, as has the idea of endowing the paradigmatic narrative of first people with obviously problematic issues regarding sexual regulation.

---

12   "The whole City, according to our Plan, was to consist of several long strait Streets, parallel to each other, with Gardens backwards, each way, and traverse Passages at proper Distances, to cross each Street, from one to the other, quite thro' the whole City". (356)

13   Daniel Cook, "Coda: Rewriting the Robinsonade", *Rewriting Crusoe: The Robinsonade across Languages, Cultures, and Media*, ed. Jakub Lipski (Lewisburg: Bucknell University Press, 2021), pp. 166.

14   Riquet, *The Aesthetics of Island Space*, p. 103.

ROBERT PALTOCK'S *PETER WILKINS* (1751)

In *Peter Wilkins*, unlike *The English Hermit*, the idea of self-discipline through sexual abstinence on the island does not appeal to the castaway. Like Philip Quarll, he is characterised by a rakish disposition in the pre-island section, where he progresses from being a spoilt mummy's boy to prematurely becoming a husband and a father through "an Intrigue with a Servant-Maid" and "frequent Conferences, in Confidence together" that put an end to his promising educational development (19–20). And, just as Quarll did not particularly struggle to find excuses for himself, and to (in his view) legitimate his subsequent relationships, so Wilkins is ready and able conveniently to kill off his wife Patty in a dream he has on the island, thus making room for his encounter with the female other.

Before this can take place, Wilkins's rakish proneness to sensual pleasure undergoes a corrective evolution on the island, where – again in a manner reminiscent of Longueville's Quarll, and very much unlike Crusoe – the castaway is characterised by a sensitivity to the beauties and fruits of the environs that was rather unusual in the early Robinsonade, which typically evaluated the natural backdrop solely with reference to its potential utility. This sensitivity, as in *The English Hermit*, is rendered with appropriate language: for instance, Wilkins "stood some time admiring" curious plants, whose "Heads rattled against each other very musically [and] made a most agreeable Sound" (86), and when he tasted new foods, including some self-made cheese, it was "the most luscious and delicate Morsel [he] ever put into [his] Lips" (89). Representations of this new, sensually receptive body stand in contrast to how the body is constructed in the pre-island narrative, not only inasmuch as they re-orientate the discourse of pleasure, but also because they offer a relief from scenes involving the imperilled and exploited body, most memorably depicted in the novel's engagement with the theme of unavoidable cannibalism, when Wilkins struggles to survive aboard a drifting boat in the company of twenty other prisoners discarded by the pirates who assaulted and ransacked the protagonist's first ship. In this episode, Paltock openly addresses what often constitutes only a shadowy presence in the Robinsonade's treatment of "going native": the castaway's transformation into a man-eater. The account of Wilkins and his company stranded on the boat offers a countdown narrative as the number of survivors gradually reduces. At one point,

> On the fifteenth day in the morning, our Carpenter, weak as he was, started up, and as the sixth Man was just dead, cut his Throat, and, whilst warm, would let out what Blood would flow; then, pulling off his old Jacket, invited us to Dinner, and cutting a large Slice off the Corpse, devoured it with as much seeming Relish, as if it had been Ox Beef. His

Example prevailed with the rest of us, one after another, to taste and eat
[...]. It has surprised me many Times since, to think how we could make
so light a Thing of eating our Fellow Creature just dead before our Eyes
[...]. (41)

As with the account of unceremonious promiscuity just described, this coarse
– in its shocking tangibility – poetics of the body subsequently gives way in the
island section to a proto-Romantic story of the idealised relationship between
the castaway and the encountered other, framed with the Edenic pleasures of
the natural world and the aestheticised eroticism previously noted. That erotic
sensuality, rather than deploying the euphemistic language of "intrigues"
and "conferences", relies on methodical reconstructions of female beauty, as
depicted in Boitard's illustrations.

Indeed, a peculiarity of *Peter Wilkins* is its language of description, which
reconciles Defoevian realist minutiae with aesthetically charged and sensual
eroticism – a reconciliation skilfully captured by Boitard's illustrations, in
which details of the machinery are complemented with the classicist, and thus
idealist, iconography of beauty. Combining imperial wonder with eroticism,
the description of Youwarkee, predictably, follows the scene of love-making
that supplies the climactic point of the island "marriage", and after which the
castaway is keen to satisfy his curiosity about his partner:

[...] at waking I was very solicitous to find out what Sort of Being I had
had in my Arms, and with what Qualities her Garment was endued, or
how contrived [...].
We rose with the Light; but surely no two were ever more amorous, or
more delighted with each other. (118)

The ensuing description of Youwarkee's graundee exemplifies the language
of bodily minutiae, which is annotated in the text with reference to Boitard's
images:

She first threw up two long Branches or Ribbs of the Whalebone [...]
which were jointed behind to the upper Bone of the Spine, and which,
when not extended, lye bent over the Shoulders, on each side of the Neck
forwards, from whence, by nearer and nearer Approaches, they just meet
at the lower Rim of the Belly, in a sort of Point; but when Extended, they
stand their whole Length above the Shoulders, not perpendicularly, but
spreading outwards, with a Webb of the softest and most playable and
springy Membrane, that can be imagined, in the Interspace between
them, reaching their Root or Joint on the Back, up above the hinder part

ROBERT PALTOCK'S *PETER WILKINS* (1751)

of the Head, and near half way their own length; but, when closed, the Membrane falls down in the Middle, upon the Neck, like an Handkerchief. [...] (138–139)

Paltock continues in this manner for a further two pages, concluding that the plates within the book will help the reader better understand what can hardly "be exprest by Words" (140) – somewhat paradoxically, given the wordiness of the account. What most certainly *is* expressed, both explicitly and implicitly, is how the machinery described, which provokes Wilkins's curiosity, simultaneously reflects the novel's erotic agenda: when deployed, the graundee discloses Youwarkee's nakedness.

The narrative zooms in on Youwarkee's naked body on two occasions: not only when the private nuptials of the couple are consummated in the castaway's grotto, but also when the account of the machinery just provided concludes with remarks on the human aspects of the Gawrey's body. Both offer conventional depictions of female beauty, tinged with sensuous enthusiasm and pseudo-scholarly realism, respectively. As for the former, we read about how "the softest Skin and most delightful Body, free from all Impediment, presented itself to [Peter's] Wishes, and gave up itself to [his] Embraces" (118), and how the castaway "command[s]" Youwarkee to satisfy his desire to see more of what is hidden beneath the machinery – "her lovely Flesh" (121). While gazing at Youwarkee's nakedness in this way, Peter both exercises his patriarchal superiority over the spouse and establishes a contrast between "Love and Curiosity" (121), with the first centring on the nakedness and the second on the machinery. This juxtaposition belongs to the larger spectrum of the novel's double voice by complicating the narrative of romantic love with imperial undertones, inherent in the aesthetics and politics of curiosity belonging to contemporary travel accounts; as Barbara Benedict points out, this also manifests itself in *Robinson Crusoe*, where the castaway "incarnates the cultural ideal of transcendent curiosity [...] as the means for power".[15] The difference in perspective is exemplified when Peter follows his detailed description of the graundee with more methodical, and less enthusiastic remarks about the winged others' physical appearance:

Tho' these People, in height, shape, and limb, very much resemble the *Europeans*, there is yet this Difference; that their Bodies are rather broader and flatter, and their Limbs, tho' as long, and well shaped, are seldom so

---

15   Barbara M. Benedict, *Curiosity: A Cultural History of Early Modern Inquiry* (Chicago and London: The University of Chicago Press, 2001), p. 109.

thick as ours [...] But their Skin, for Beauty and Fairness, exceeds ours very much. (141)

Peter's fascination with Youwarkee, which lies at the core of their androgynous relationship, is thus ambiguous, oscillating between or combining sensual responsiveness, the male gaze and an aesthetic of imperial curiosity. Boitard's visuals, in this respect, constitute a multi-functional addition: they support the sensual observations with their idealist iconography, foreground Wilkins's perspective by the figures' postures, and underline the documentary quality of the narrative of exploration. As David Fausett points out, such "visual evidence" in "an age of empiricism, science, discovery and technological innovation" was taken "as a criterion of truth and value".[16]

The unity of Peter and Youwarkee's bodies is most fully realised through their offspring, who can be read as embodiments of the novel's fantasy of miscegenation. The theme of racial intermarriage, as Roxann Wheeler explains, gained in importance in the mid-eighteenth-century novel, even superseding the "master/slave dynamic", as the imperial concerns of the time moved from the politics of conquest to "issues of governance".[17] But these concerns were already topical in Defoe's time: they feature extensively in *The Farther Adventures* and its complex treatment of island ordering through marriages with the native women, including the re-enactment of the Crusoe/Friday encounter in Will Atkins's relationship with his indigenous wife. In *Peter Wilkins*, the emphasis is not so much on the racial and cultural difference of the spouses, as on the effects of miscegenation on the offspring. Wilkins is characteristically highly meticulous in explaining the bodily form of his children, and what they take after from both father and mother:

> I had now lived here almost fourteen Years; and besides the three Sons before-mentioned, had three Girls and one Boy. *Pedro*, my eldest, had the *Graundee*, but too small to be useful; my second Son, *Tommy*, had it compleat; so had my three Daughters; but *Jemmy* and *David*, the youngest Sons, none at all. [...]
>
> And what is very remarkable in my Children, is, that my three Daughters and *Tommy*, who had the full *Graundee*, had exactly their Mother's Sight, *Jemmy* and *David* had just my Sight, and *Pedro*'s Sight was between both [...]. (160–161)

---

16   Fausett, *Images of the Antipodes in the Eighteenth Century*, p. 79.
17   Wheeler, *The Complexion of Race*, p. 147.

ROBERT PALTOCK'S *PETER WILKINS* (1751)

The naivety of Wilkins's theory of hybridisation is perhaps understandable given the period context, but it is significant that the careful ordering of evolutionary change based on who the children take after is not a coherent discursive strategy for establishing separate lines of gendered legacy. On the one hand, the fact that the three daughters do not take after their father at all may suggest a patriarchal allegory of inheritance, whereby the daughters cannot place themselves in the father's line; on the other, the sons display various bodily constitutions, suggesting that the merger between the castaway and the other relies on accidental – genetic, we would now say – configuration. The most interesting case, of course, is the first-born Pedro – a complete hybrid, who looks like a combination of both parents, and whose graundee is a mere embellishment. His eyesight, however, is not affected by light, as is the case of all glumms and gawreys used to living in perpetual twilight and the four children of Wilkins who take after their mother and have developed a complete graundee. The first-born is naturally first in the line of succession, so his faulty graundee tones down the optimism of miscegenation, suggesting that the traits inherited from the other may serve no useful purpose, but nevertheless remain a lasting sign of difference. *Peter Wilkins* does indeed add to a relatively extensive corpus of interracial romance in English texts that developed from the seventeenth century onwards, and which depicted the relationship "often sympathetically", as Susan B. Iwanisziw puts it.[18] But in doing so, it problematises the "sympathy" that was typical of eighteenth-century abolitionist writing, and also characterised *The Farther Adventures*, with hints that – even if not "coarse" or "depreciative", as Iwanisziw dubs the alternatives to sympathy[19] – are at least ambiguous.

The ambiguous valuation of miscegenist hybridisation was elaborated upon in an early imitation of *Peter Wilkins*: *A Narrative of the Life and Astonishing Adventures of John Daniel* written by Ralph Morris and published in 1751. In this Robinsonade, at one point the eponymous castaway is confronted with hybrid creatures, whose bodily form had been determined through their castaway mother's adulterous union with a sea monster. The story of hybridisation is thus framed with a quasi-religious account of a fallen woman, reminiscent – as it were – of witch-trial confessions: "I Joanna Anderson, a child of hell, and

---

18   Susan B. Iwanisziw, "Intermarriage in Late-Eighteenth-Century British Literature: Currents in Assimilation and Exclusion", *Eighteenth-Century Life* 31.2 (2007): 56.

19   Iwanisziw, "Intermarriage in Late-Eighteenth-Century British Literature", p. 56.

60 CHAPTER 3

companion of demons",[20] "entered into criminal commerce" with a monster and gave birth to the pair now encountered by Daniel:

> they bore the exact resemblance of the human species in their erect posture and limbs, save their mouths were as broad as their whole faces, and had very little chins; their arms seemed all bone, and very thin, their hands had very long fingers, and webbed between, with long claws on them, and their feet were just the same, with very little heel; their legs and thighs long, and strait, with strong scales on them, and the other parts of their bodies were exactly human, but covered with the same hair as a seal.[21]

This description, in a manner analogical to *Peter Wilkins*, is accompanied by illustrations, also by Louis-Philippe Boitard, which complement this fictionalisation of human-animal hybridisation with a racist agenda. In Boitard's illustrations (Figure 11) the human-animal beings are clearly racial others, with fishy characteristics, such as the mouth or the scales, used as indicators of racial difference, thus concretising Morris's allegory of miscegenation. As Weaver-Hightower points out, *John Daniel*'s hybrids are projections of "colonial fears of miscegenation [...], 'unnatural' love [...] and degeneration".[22]

At the same time, the narrative parallels the implication found in *Peter Wilkins*, that however transgressive a relationship with the encountered other might appear to be, it can nevertheless be seen as a sensible option, prompting a change conducive to survival. In Daniel's words:

> [...] suppose you had been like me, could you have supplied the wants, or sustained the horrors of this loansome habitation with equal pleasure, as you now can? If not, how happy are you in your present form? Wholly applicable to the life designed for you? And I see no reason, but having been a meer man, you should (in this retirement) have lamented your misfortune, of not having parts and capacities, proper for the lot you was fallen into.[23]

Whatever the effect in aesthetic terms, hybridisation is thus represented as indispensable for the castaways' life on the island; this idea is underlined

---

20   Ralph Morris, *A Narrative of the Life and Astonishing Adventures of John Daniel* (London: Printed for M. Cooper, 1751), p. 258.
21   Morris, *John Daniel*, pp. 221–222.
22   Weaver-Hightower, *Empire Islands*, p. 155.
23   Morris, *John Daniel*, p. 244.

FIGURE 11 Louis-Philippe Boitard, the illustration of the male hybrid from Ralph Morris's *John Daniel* (1751), from the 1926 edition (London: Holden)
COURTESY OF THE UNIVERSITY OF MICHIGAN LIBRARY, SPECIAL COLLECTIONS RESEARCH CENTRE

in *Peter Wilkins*, where it is Youwarkee's skills that enable the pair to sustain themselves.

Wilkins and Youwarkee's relationship, accordingly, does not depend solely on the union of the bodies (captured literally in the love-making scenes and metaphorically through their hybrid offspring), but also on the unity of their minds and efforts. The effect is a fantasy of family utopia, foreshadowing later group Robinsonades, such as *The Swiss Family Robinson* by Johann David Wyss (1812) , and correctively engaging with Defoe's model.[24] Like Crusoe, Wilkins teaches Youwarkee English but also learns her native tongue; as he lacks her abilities, she is the one responsible for retrieving goods from the wreck of the ship; he converts her to Christianity, but finds it relatively easy given her "Notion of a supreme Power", albeit "confused" (156); they divide the labour, with their unique predispositions determining their occupation. Wilkins meets her family, but unlike Crusoe's encounter with Friday's father, his meeting with Youwarkee's brother is between equals, with two erect bodies, in contrast to the prostrated bodies of Defoe's others: "I rose up, and taking him by the Right-hand, lifted it to my Lips, and kissed it. He likewise immediately stood up, and we embraced each other with great Tenderness" (178). Finally, she does not merely accompany Peter in leaving the island: she is indirectly responsible for their rescue.

By inverting the fairy-tale rescue narrative, the family utopia section of *Peter Wilkins* inevitably ponders gender issues, in as much as it fictionalises a female character somewhere between the "rescued" other and the "rescuing" redeemer, who is at the same time a female castaway, active in her sustenance and survival. Youwarkee performs a number of "masculine" chores, as suggested, while Wilkins embraces "feminine" domesticity whenever the winged Gawrey ventures from the home, as she is – literally – equipped to do so. On the level of discourse, the gender binary is resolved when what the pair say to one another, and their choice of words, undermines the conventional parameters of femininity and masculinity. For instance, when Youwarkee and three of the "graundeed" children set out for her homeland to pay a visit to her father, it is she who takes the risk, and it is Wilkins who remains at home and worries: "I can't say [...] that I was perfectly easy when they were gone; for my Affection for them all would work up imaginary Fears, too potent for my Reason to

---

24 As Peter Hulme points out, the colonialist agenda of Friday's education depends on a curious construction, or "production", of his ignorance, as Crusoe teaches him how to barbeque and deal with a canoe – that is, things that Europeans learned from Carib culture. See Peter Hulme, *Colonial Encounters: Europe and the Native Caribbean, 1492–1797* (London and New York: Methuen, 1986), pp. 210–211.

ROBERT PALTOCK'S *PETER WILKINS* (1751) 63

dispel" (169). It is also Wilkins who, during the period of Youwarkee's absence, takes care of the other children and performs household chores, including redecorating the house ready to host his wife's father: "we employed ourselves within Doors, in preparing several Things, which might not only be useful and ornamental, if the old *Glumm* should come to see us, but might also divert us, and make the Time pass less tediously" (169). A conceptual link between domesticity and boredom clearly reflects how Wilkins accommodates femininity while Youwarkee exercises her "masculine" need for mobility.

The gender binary is also challenged when the issue of clothing comes to the fore. As discussed in Chapter 1, in *Robinson Crusoe*, shortly after the castaway "saves" Friday, for some reason the other "seem'd very glad" to be receiving clothes from Crusoe, at least from the latter's perspective. Friday's presupposed desire to imitate his "master's" appearance, later reiterated in his declaration that his people "are willing love learn" from Robinson, is an imperialist projection of colonial mimicry, as Homi Bhabha would have it, which assumes that the colonised want to imitate the coloniser.[25] Youwarkee, too, though her relationship with Wilkins is not a straightforward adaptation of Defoe's master-servant pattern, expresses a desire to mimic the Westerner: "I will make me a Coat, like yours, says she, for I don't like to look different from my dear Husband and Children" (142). Given what Dror Wahrman aptly describes as the eighteenth-century "literalness [...]with which dress was taken to make identity, rather than merely to signify its anterior existence",[26] the fantasy of an androgynous relationship now seems too transgressive to Wilkins: "No *Youwarkee*, replied I, you must not do so; if you make such a Jacket as mine, there will be no Distinction between *Glumm* and *Gawry*" (142). Hagglund and Laidlow have pointed out that Wilkins is anxious about his idealised relationship with Youwarkee in as much as it subverts "his assertions of European masculinity".[27] I would argue that Wilkins is ready to re-envision how masculinity and femininity are typically constructed, as seen in his progressive attitude towards the issues of labour and agency, but that this does not necessarily translate into a readiness fundamentally to revise the male-female divide; Wilkins is adamant that the traditional sartorial markers – or more appropriately, the constituents of gender – remain in place.

---

25   Homi K. Bhabha, *The Location of Culture* (London and New York: Routledge, 1994), pp. 85–92.

26   Dror Wahrman, *The Making of the Modern Self: Identity and Culture in Eighteenth-Century England* (New Haven: Yale University Press, 2004), pp. 177–178.

27   Hagglund and Laidlow, "'A Man might find every thing in your Country'", p. 146.

It is also dress that eventually indicates the gawry's change, prompted by her exposure to Englishness. During the anticipated family meeting, the couple delight in a stratagem against Youwarkee's father, Pendlehamby, and her sister, Hallycarnie, based on the family members' inability to recognise Wilkins's beloved in "her *English* Gown", which hides the graundee (207). This takes place at the beginning Volume II, where the narrative is about to move the emphasis from family life to Wilkins's political activism in Doorpt Swangeantine. There, however appreciative of some of the native people's civilisational ideas, including – in a truly proto-ecological manner – food and energy economies,[28] Peter nevertheless lives up to the role expected of an imperialist. This ordering of the ideological double voice is foreshadowed in the family life section by Wilkins's performative display of his dressed and disciplined body, the change in which is underlined by the difficulty Youwarkee has in recognising him:

> I was dressed in a Cinnamon-coloured Gold-button Coat, Scarlet Waistcoat, Velvet Breeches, white Silk Stockings, the Campain-wig flowing, a Gold-laced Hat and Feather, Point Cravat, Silver Sword, and over all my Cloak. [...]
>
> Poor *Youwarkee*, who knew nothing of my Dress, or of the Loss of my Beard [which he had shaved], was Thunderstruck when she saw me, not being able to observe any Visage I had, for my great Wig, and Hat. [...] I sitting as great as a Lord, till they came within about thirty Paces of my Seat; and then gravely rising, I pulled off my Hat, and made my Obeisance [...]. (204–206)

There are hints at Peter's effeminacy as he anxiously awaits the family visit and weighs up the various possibilities for how he should look, hesitating over whether to shave or not. However, eventually he transforms from being a domesticated spouse who takes care of the children and his looks alike into a "Lord" who welcomes Youwarkee's family into his dominions.

The novel's fantasy of hybridisation, with the gender binary now reinstated and the androgynous ideal somehow abandoned, returns to the question of the graundee. This time, however, it does not feature as a crucial element of Wilkins and Youwarkee's miscegenist union and its embodied results, but as an indicator of desired and eventually appropriated otherness. Wilkins effectively needs a graundee in order to carry out his colonial mission in Doorpt Swangeanti, and since he cannot partake in the evolutionary change himself,

---

28 The winged people live in harmony with their environment: they only eat what grows on trees and bushes; they do not produce energy, relying on hot springs of varying temperatures; and they use luminescent flies as sources of light.

ROBERT PALTOCK'S *PETER WILKINS* (1751)

unlike his offspring, he designs a substitute: a flying machine. This machine, which is in fact a kind of sedan chair to be lifted from the ground, is meticulously described, establishing a parallel between the language used to account for Youwarkee's graundee and that which describes Peter's metaphorical transformation:

> I pitched upon a strong broad Board [...] about twelve Feet long, and a Foot and half broad: Upon the middle of which, I nailed down one of my Chairs. Then I took one Cord of about thirty-four Feet long, making Handloops at each End, and nailed it down in the Middle to the under Side of my Board, as near as I could to the fore End of it; and I took another Cord of the same Length and Make, and this, I nailed within three Feet of the further End of my Board. I then took a Cord of about twenty Feet long, and nailed about three Feet behind the foremost, and a fourth of the same Length, and the further End of my Board; by which Means, the first and third Ropes being the longest, and at such a Distance from the short Ropes, the Glumms who held them, would fly so much higher and forwarder than the short Rope ones, that they and their Ropes would be quite out of the others way; which would not have happened, if either the Ropes had been all of one Length, or nearer to, or farther from one another: And then considering that if I should receive a sudden Jerk or Twitch, I might possibly be shook off my Chair, I took a smaller Rope to tie myself with fast to the Chair; and then I was sure if I fell into the Sea, I should at least have the Board and Chair with me, which might possibly buoy me up, till the Glumms could descend to my Assistance. (248–249)

Like the graundee, Wilkins's flying sedan chair is also, in a way, designed for the water; the parallelism is therefore indicated at the discursive level of description and by the chair's intended functionality. At both levels, the juxtaposition clearly favours the graundee, which is described in a more imaginative and aesthetically refined manner and relies on "natural" and autonomous functioning. The potential aquatic use of Wilkins's chair is merely an alternative designed to facilitate rescue, suggesting that the experienced protagonist remains mindful of the prospective castaway scenarios in which he may feature, while the flying depends on Youwarkee's countrymen holding onto the ropes. A form of appreciation and a material token of what he lacks, Wilkins's flying machine nevertheless becomes an embodiment of his imperial rule, given the obvious connotations a sedan chair evokes for both the carriers and the carried. The transformation of Wilkins's body through the metaphorical incorporation of the flying machine, from a deficient to an overgrown body seen to be as one with this symbol of imperial rule, is most potently rendered when Wilkins – now a reformer in Youwarkee's country – sits on his chair and supervises a battle between the governmental forces (which he supports) and a group of rebels. Wilkins gives a detailed account of his posture, and of the arrangement of cannons and rifles at his disposal. In a manner reminiscent of Crusoe's second character sketch, in which the heavily armed castaway is ready to defend "his" island, the scene features Wilkins as an embodiment of imperial masculinity: sitting on a throne of sorts, leading an army, and surrounded with weapons. Predictably, the battle ends with Wilkins's Indiana-Jones-like shooting of Harlokin, the leader of the rebels.

The scene was skilfully illustrated by Boitard (Figure 12), whose changes to the textual description elaborate on the novel's colonial undertones, which gather momentum in Volume II. The boards that enable Wilkins's method of flying are here placed on the ground, recalling the royal carpets placed beneath a throne. In representing the protagonist in this way Boitard alludes to portraits of the nobility that typically drew attention to the groin to emphasise aristocratic ideas of progeny and patrilineage. Accordingly, rather than place three muskets at either of Wilkins's sides, Boitard equips the protagonist with one rifle, held vertically between the widely spread legs, a clearly phallic symbol that stands for colonial rule. There is a truly epic quality to the battle of the Glumms, their bodies consistently represented like classical sculptures and displaying inherent nobility, but given Wilkins's posture and the incorporated weaponry, the established power dynamic is clear.

Peter Wilkins exemplifies the polyphonic quality that Mikhail Bakhtin believed to have supplied the richness of the novel as a genre. It offers a unique blend of, at times, contradictory ideological voices, with an ambiguous problematisation of the interracial encounter and gender binaries at the text's centre. While the colonial voice eventually surfaces and dominates, in a very similar fashion to *The English Hermit*, its sound is never fully cleared of the subversive, counter-imperial echoes, suggesting a more complex understanding of gender and race. This indicates why some early nineteenth-century readers considered that it appeared to be ahead of its time. As with *The English Hermit*, and even with *Crusoe*, the castaway's body becomes a discursive space where these voices are tested against one another. But Paltock goes beyond the castaway, whose metamorphoses remain largely metaphorical, and constructs an inter-character, and interracial, somatic network, where the bodies of the protagonist, the other and their offspring are interrelated in producing the novel's complex meanings.

The 1750s have been recognised in eighteenth-century criticism not only as a decade of metafictional experimentation, leading up to Laurence Sterne's

FIGURE 12   Louis-Philippe Boitard, *Nasgigs Engagement with Harlokins General*, an illustration to Robert Paltock's *Peter Wilkins* (1751)
THE PUBLIC DOMAIN REVIEW

Tristram Shandy, but also as a time when authors and publishers of fiction manifested a profound understanding of the material aspects of book production.[29] *Peter Wilkins* testifies to this in how its meanings are visually concretised by illustrations. They are crucial in foregrounding the body and its discursive character as represented in the novel, but also reveal the illustrator's own initiative in further complicating Paltock's take on embodiment through distinctly visual means (such as perspective and iconographic choices), but also through subtle modifications, as revealed in the final element of the set, creating a unique tension produced by the verbal and the textualised visual.

29   See Christina Lupton, "Giving Power to the Medium: Recovering the 1750s", *The Eighteenth Century* 52.3/4 (2011): 289–302.

CHAPTER 4

The Female American (1767): a Failed Amazon

Robinsonades featuring a female castaway appeared shortly after *Robinson Crusoe* itself. In Ambrose Evans's *The Adventures and Surprizing Deliverances of James Dubourdieu and His Wife*, published in October 1719, the heroine is appropriately placed alongside her attentive husband, though the narrative is much more concerned with describing the indigenous society than the promised "adventures" of the marooned couple. Penelope Aubin, in *The Strange Adventures of the Count de Vinevil* of 1721, strands one Ardelisa, accompanied by "Violetta, a Venetian Lady, the Captain of the Ship, a Priest, and five Sailors", while in *The Life of Charlotta Du Pont* (1723), she has the eponymous protagonist shipwrecked in the company of "several Gentlemen and Ladys", as the full titles of these works inform us. Such texts, as C. M. Owen has demonstrated, merit attention as hybrid constructs reconciling conservative values with subversive and anti-patriarchal ideas, implied by an open destabilisation of the ideal of feminine domesticity.[1] Indeed, as Unca Eliza, the first-person narrator of *The Female American* (1767), has it:

> The lives of women being commonly domestick, the occurrences of them are generally pretty nearly of the same kind; whilst those of men, frequently more vagrant, subject them often to experience greater vicissitudes, many times wonderful and strange. Though a woman, it has been my lot to have experienced much of the latter [...].[2]

That said, such examples fell far short of fully exploring the subversive potential inherent in the female Robinsonade, whereby an isolated woman or a group of women not only leave the "domestick" space, as Unca Eliza recognises, but also survive and conquer both the island and what are conventionally perceived to be the limitations of the female body. In this, these eighteenth-century texts differ from more recent examples, which have gone beyond "wonderful and strange" adventures. Ian Kinane, discussing twentieth- and twenty-first-century developments in the genre, claims that "the increase in female writers adopting

---

1 C. M. Owen, *The Female Crusoe: Hybridity, Trade and the Eighteenth-Century Individual* (Amsterdam and New York: Rodopi, 2010).

2 *The Female American; Or, The Adventures of Unca Eliza Winkfield*, ed. Michelle Burnham and James Freitas (Peterborough: Broadview, 2014), p. 45. Further references to *The Female American* will be parenthetical.

© KONINKLIJKE BRILL NV, LEIDEN, 2024 | DOI:10.1163/9789004692916_006

the Robinsonade form [and featuring female castaways] suggests that the genre has begun to move further away from its imperialist, masculinist origins".[3] One way in which this has been achieved has been through liberating the female body from the patriarchal constraints on sexuality and agency. A case in point is Libba Bray's *Beauty Queens* of 2011, which, by stranding teen beauty contestants on an island, metaphorically tears them away from the patriarchal logic of gaze and display and plays with the Amazonian myth of dangerous femininity. As Amy Hicks argues, the island in this novel becomes "a distinctly experimental arena for girls to navigate gendered behaviours and question conservative social mores concerning female sexuality".[4] The prefatory warning in "A Word from Your Sponsor" opening the book – "If you should happen to notice anything suspicious in the coming pages, do alert the proper authorities" – is an ironic foreshadowing of subversive content, such as when one of the girls dreams about the other being "The Queen of the Amazons".[5] These sentiments are also captured on the book's cover, where the beauty contest sash worn by a scantily-clad woman is doubled by an ammunition belt loaded with lipsticks.[6]

In this relatively rich tradition of Robinsonades featuring women castaways,[7] the eighteenth-century text that has garnered considerable critical attention in the last two decades is *The Female American*, which sees half-"Indian" and half-English Unca Eliza marooned on an American island as punishment for not being willing to sign a marriage contract with the captain's son. She survives following the written advice that she discovers, produced by her solitary predecessor on the island, a hermit whose life in isolation, as well as his "follies" and "vices" before the shipwreck (80), reveal at least several parallels with the life of Longueville's protagonist. Indeed, Unca mentions "read[ing] of hermits" (66), and while *The English Hermit* was not the only narrative of this type available at the time, according to the English Short Title Catalogue the 1750s and 1760s saw the publication of several new editions of this novel after two decades of relative obscurity, so it is possible that the anonymous author of *The Female American* was elaborating on this model.

---

3   Ian Kinane, "Introduction: The Robinsonade Genre an the Didactic Impulse", *Didactics and the Modern Robinsonade*, ed. Ian Kinane (Liverpool: Liverpool University Press, 2019), p. 35.

4   Amy Hicks, "Romance, the Robinsonade, and the Cultivation of Adolescent Female Desire in Libba Bray's *Beauty Queens*", *Didactics and the Modern Robinsonade*, ed. Ian Kinane (Liverpool: Liverpool University Press, 2019), pp. 185–186.

5   Libba Bray, *Beauty Queens* (Crows Nest: Allen & Unwin, 2011), pp. 1, 173.

6   See https://libbabray.com/books/beauty-queens/.

7   An extremely useful bibliographic tool to research the female Robinsonades is the database compiled by Anne Birgitte Rønning, which includes international examples from the eighteenth and nineteenth centuries (2011–2020). https://www2.hf.uio.no/tjenester/bibliografi /Robinsonades.

Having made herself at home on the island, Unca colonises the native people by converting them to Christianity. To facilitate this, she uses a monumental solar idol, which she ascends and speaks from to subjugate the confounded locals. One of the commands this Christianised oracle issues to the gathered believers is that they must obey unconditionally a woman who will one day appear on the island, which guarantees that Unca – who, thanks to her origins, speaks the native language – remains safe among them and can even play the role of spiritual leader. Finally, in a rather anti-romantic climax, she marries her cousin, who comes to her rescue, and the couple remain in the New World to continue their missionary work.

The Female American met with moderate interest upon publication and was not held in high regard. A short summary in the *Monthly Review* considers it "a sort of second *Robinson Crusoe*; full of wonders", while the reader for *The Critical Review* is not amused and wishes the author would have "saved us six hours very disagreeable employment".[8] The novel was not reissued until 1800, when an illustrated edition appeared in Newburyport, Massachusetts, thereby confirming the suggestion made by *The Critical Review*'s commentator that the novel would have been more successful and popular with readers in America. Things have changed, and in the last two decades *The Female American* has received substantial scholarly attention, realising the hope expressed by Michelle Burnham and James Freitas (who prepared the 2014 Broadview edition) that the novel should become "a more widely read and studied text".[9] One indicator of this text's newfound critical status is that in 2016 a special issue of *Women's Studies* was entirely dedicated to it, addressing a wide array of topics including "genre convention, the role of the domestic sphere, identity construction, religious conversion, and social justice".[10] Building on this critical work, and adding to existing discussions of the novel's indebtedness to the traditional imperial message despite its seemingly progressive agenda,[11] this

---

8   See *Appendix E: Reviews of The Female American*, *The Female American*, p. 249.

9   Michelle Burnham and James Freitas, "A Note on the Text", *The Female American*, p. 40.

10   Jesslyn Collins-Frohlich and Denise Mary MacNeil, "Introduction." *Women's Studies* 45:7 (2016): 612.

11   Chloe Wigston Smith, "The Empire of Home: Global Domestic Objects and *The Female American* (1767)", *Journal for Eighteenth-Century Studies* 40.1 (2017): 67–87; Przemysław Uściński, "Castaways and Colonialism: Dislocating Cultural Encounter in *The Female American* (1767)", *Rewriting Crusoe: The Robinsonade across Languages, Cultures, and Media*, ed. Jakub Lipski (Lewisburg: Bucknell University Press, 2020), pp. 39–51; Emelia Abbé, "Collecting and Collected: Native American Subjectivity and Transatlantic Transactions in *The Female American*", *Early American Literature* 54.1 (2019): 37–67.

THE FEMALE AMERICAN (1767): A FAILED AMAZON   71

chapter concentrates on the myth of the Amazon as representing the unreal-
ised potential of *The Female American.*

The myth has been seen as central from the perspective of feminist literary
theory. Despite its possible origin as a male-created story warning against the
threat of dangerous "bad girls", it has been appropriated from this misogynist
imagery and recontextualised as a myth of female strength and independence.[12] As Abby Wettan Kleinbaum explains, the Amazon has been viewed as
a feminist model of "political power, of military prowess, and [...] autonomy
and hence dignity".[13] The myth, however, is rarely invoked in studies of the
eighteenth-century Robinsonade, despite some fine work on the Amazon in
eighteenth-century fiction more broadly.[14] Julie Wheelwright identifies more
than one hundred "female warriors" in early eighteenth-century literary texts,[15]
and Laura Brown shows the persistence of the representation of "the strutting
Amazonian Whore" from Juvenal's sixth satire, as translated by John Dryden.[16]
Notable fictions featuring Amazons in the period include Alexander Pope's *The
Rape of the Lock* (1712–17), Defoe's *The Fortunate Mistress* (1724) or *The Female
Soldier; Or, The Surprising Life and Adventures of Hannah Snell* (1750), by an
anonymous author. For some reason, despite the possible Defoevian allusion
in the title of the last of these works, the form of the Robinsonade was not
considered the appropriate background for the staging of an Amazon. Quite
tellingly, when Owen refers to the myth in her discussion of "female Crusoes"
in the eighteenth century, the text under scrutiny is *The Fortunate Mistress* by
virtue of Roxana's affinities with Defoe's castaway.[17]

When Terry Castle discussed the masquerade as a potential utopia of female
sovereignty, she showed how it "engendered an 'Amazonian race'", a society of
"women unmarked by patriarchy".[18] The utopian or heterotopic implications
of the Robinsonade and its islands could have provided a perfect framework

---

12   Sigrid King, "Amazon", *Encyclopedia of Feminist Literary Theory*, ed. Elizabeth Kowaleski
      Wallace (London and New York: Routledge, 2009), pp. 16–17.
13   Abby Wettan Kleinbaum, *The War against the Amazons* (New York: McGraw-Hill, 1983),
      p. 224.
14   Laura Brown, *Ends of Empire: Women and Ideology in Early Eighteenth-Century English Lit-
      erature* (Ithaca, NY, and London: Cornell University Press, 1993); Wahrman, *The Making
      of the Modern Self*, pp. 3–29; Laura Linker, *Dangerous Women, Libertine Epicures, and the
      Rise of Sensibility, 1670–1730* (Farnham: Ashgate, 2011), pp. 115–140.
15   Julie Wheelwright, *Amazons and Military Maids: Women Who Dressed as Men in Pursuit of
      Life, Liberty and Happiness* (London: Pandora, 1989), p. 8.
16   Brown, *Ends of Empire*, p. 138.
17   Owen, *Female Crusoes*, pp. 89–93.
18   Terry Castle, *Masquerade and Civilisation: The Carnivalesque in Eighteenth-Century
      English Culture and Fiction* (Stanford: Stanford University Press, 1986), p. 255.

for this kind of narrative, but these possibilities were not fully embraced in the eighteenth century. The text arguably the closest to doing so, *Hannah Hewit* of 1792, was written by Charles Dibdin, a man who believed that "the idea of a female Crusoe would excite curiosity", but who nevertheless admitted to having based the heroine on his brother, who was lost at sea.[19] Accordingly, Dibdin introduces the heroine in the prefatory section: "Her intellects were strong, her invention prompt, and her conclusions sound and just. Added to exquisite feminine susceptibility, she had a male mind".[20] He thus corrects, in a sense, the Amazonian ideal of prowess and independence with the notion of the "male mind", which, however, is not put forward with reference to her survival on the island but to her authorship of the autobiographical narrative, which was in fact written by the male "editor" of the supposedly found manuscript.

In *The Female American*, in turn, the idea of a "female Crusoe" is much more than a curiosity, and the heroine's Amazonian potential bears its original mythical significance, being both explored and abandoned as such. Unca Eliza's hybrid body is a space inscribed by conflicted discourses that the novel juxtaposes, creating an ideological double voice reminiscent of the other body-centred narratives discussed in this book. Following Owen's idea of the eighteenth-century female Robinsonade as a space of ideological ambiguity, I will complicate too-optimistic readings of *The Female American*'s progressivism, which interpret the novel as "an irresistible antidote" to the "masculine individualism and female domesticity" that dominated eighteenth-century fiction,[21] and which have read the heroine's "ambiguously racialised and gendered bodily and cultural self" as an assertion of "the flexibly gendered, multiracial, multicultural, multilingual, and pan-Atlantic (or regional) woman [...] capable of influencing outcomes among civilisations".[22] While such sentiments are clearly part of the novel's message,[23] and are suggestively embodied

---

19   Charles Dibdin, *The Professional Life of Mr. C. Dibdin*. Vol. 3 (London: Published by the Author), p. 319.

20   Charles Dibdin, *Hannah Hewit* (London: Printed for Charles Dibdin, 1792), p. VI.

21   Mary Helen McMurran, "Realism and the Unreal in *The Female American*", *The Eighteenth Century*, 52.3/4 (2011), p. 324.

22   Denise Mary MacNeil, "Empire and the Pan-Atlantic Self in *The Female American; or, The Adventures of Unca Eliza Winkfield*", *Women's Narratives of the Early Americas and the Formation of Empire*, ed. Mary McAleer Balkun and Susan C. Imbarrato (New York: Palgrave Macmillan, 2016), p. 110.

23   Alexis McQuigge offers a balanced reading of how the novel reconciles conservative values with progressive "moments" of female empowerment. Alexis McQuigge, "'That Person Shall be a Woman': Matriarchal Authority and the Fantasy of Female Power in *The Female American*", *Transatlantic Women Travelers, 1688–1843*, ed. Misty Krueger (Lewisburg: Bucknell University Press, 2021), pp. 131–143.

THE FEMALE AMERICAN (1767): A FAILED AMAZON   73

by the heroine's Amazonian appearance, I will also show how they are eventually compromised by Unca Eliza's submission to imperialist and patriarchal demands.

The Female American signals its dependence on the Amazonian myth from the very outset of the narrative, which establishes the family background of Unca Eliza and sketches her appearance. The heroine is a fruit of a Pocahontas-Smith-like relationship,[24] narrated in the first two chapters of the novel, and distinguishes herself through her unconventional appearance:

> My tawny complexion, and the oddity of my dress, attracted every one's attention, for my mother used to dress me in a kind of mixed habit, neither perfectly in the Indian, nor yet in the European taste, either of fine white linen, or a rich silk. I never wore a cap; but my lank black hair was adorned with diamonds and flowers. In the winter I wore a kind of loose mantle or cloak, which I used occasionally to wear on one shoulder, or to cast it behind me in folds, tied in the middle with a ribband, which gave it a pleasing kind of romantic air. My arms were also adorned with strings of diamonds, and one of the same kind surrounded my waist. I frequently diverted myself with wearing the bow and arrow the queen my aunt left me, and was so dexterous a shooter, that, when very young, I could shoot a bird on the wing. (58)

Thus, after suggesting a complex gender identity at the beginning of her account, when she highlights the "masculine" character of her adventures, Unca now underlines her racial and cultural hybridity, represented by her "tawny complexion" – which, let us recall, was termed "ugly" in Defoe's sketch of Friday – and her "mixed habit". The typical Amazonian props – the bow and arrows – gain in significance not only as a memento of her indigenous origin but also as an indicator of matrilineal ancestry, as Scarlett Bowen has demonstrated,[25] and which is central to the challenge that she poses to the patriarchal system: "I would never marry any man who could not use a bow and arrow as well as I could" (60). The bow and arrows that she inherited from her late aunt indicate her Amazonian dignity, but also the inherent "savagery" of female anger: the aunt, in love with Unca's father, at one point attempted

---

24   For a reading of Unca Eliza as a Pocahontas figure, see Betty Joseph, "Re(playing) Crusoe/ Pocahontas: Circum-Atlantic Stagings in *The Female American*", *Criticism* 42.3 (2000): 317–335.

25   Scarlett Bowen, "Via Media: Transatlantic Anglicanism in *The Female American*", *The Eighteenth Century* 53.2 (2012): 201.

to murder him for not reciprocating her feelings. This tinge of "savagery" imprinted on Unca's bodily constitution is not particularly countered by her English father, who remains largely absent, but by her uncle, who undertakes her classical and religious education. In this way, Unca's hybrid identity is represented as having been formed by her aunt and uncle, standing for the indigenous and English components of her selfhood, and the ideological double voice of the novel in general.

The paradox underpinning the narrative, which decides the failure of Unca's Amazonian potential, is that the heroine's re-enactment of the myth is largely confined to domestic and familiar spaces, where her difference as a racial and cultural hybrid and the shadowy presence of her aunt become sources of empowerment. She "diverts" herself with using her bow in a ruthless manner ("I could shoot a bird on the wing" [58]), but she enjoys being treated "in a degree little inferior to that of a princess" (58), declining proposals of marriage and entertaining herself at her admirers' expense (59) – including her cousin, whose courtship meets with laughter and retorts "in the Indian language, of which he was entirely ignorant" (60). Unca's defiance of patriarchal rule eventually puts her life at risk when she staunchly refuses to sign a marriage contract with the son of her own ship's captain, resulting in her being marooned on a desert island where the villain hopes she will be "a prey to wild beasts" (63).

The beginning of the island section looks promising: Unca urges the captain to let her keep the bow and arrows, thus reasserting her identity as defined at the outset of the novel. Allowing the heroine conveniently to keep the Amazonian weapon has obvious narrative consequences as far as the reader's expectations are concerned: the bow and arrows will both protect and sustain the castaway. The frontispiece to the 1800 edition (Figure 13), depicting Unca Eliza in line with how she is represented in the character sketch quoted above, fuels these expectations. It shows the protagonist against a natural backdrop, in her "mixed habit" and using her bow, which suggests that it is showing the castaway struggling for her survival, in a manner reminiscent of the other Robinsonade frontispieces discussed in this book. But the scene visualised features Unca "diverting" herself in the homely context, perhaps by targeting birds (also depicted); it does not belong to the narrative of her "extraordinary adventures" (as the subtitle of this edition has it).

In fact, the island narrative in *The Female American* makes absolutely no mention of Unca's use of her weapon; indeed, the next time it is referred to is when it serves a merely decorative function, when she anticipates meeting the locals she has manipulated, "with [her] bow and arrows hung over [her] shoulders" (122). Instead, from the moment she is cast away, Unca Eliza is redefined within the patriarchal frames of conventional femininity: "Thus disconsolate, and alone, I sat on the sea-shore. My grief was too great for my

THE FEMALE AMERICAN (1767): A FAILED AMAZON

FIGURE 13   The frontispiece to the 1800 edition of *The Female American* (Newburyport: Angier March)
COURTESY OF BEINECKE RARE BOOK AND MANUSCRIPT LIBRARY, YALE UNIVERSITY

76 CHAPTER 4

spirits to bear; I sunk in a swoon on the ground" (65). The body of a weaponed Amazon, erect and ready to exercise its agency, transforms into a "senseless" (65), horizontal body on the ground: immobile, passive, subject to a conventionally feminine "swoon". Unca "swoons" repeatedly on the island, thus fitting into the typified image of the hysterical female body as represented in contemporaneous medical and novelistic discourse.[26] While Ildiko Csengei has demonstrated that some sentimental fiction by women challenged this stereotypical understanding of swooning, investing the reaction and its literary representations with subversive messages – such as those implying sexual desire or forms of protest[27] – the account of Unca's bodily weakness in *The Female American* follows patriarchal clichés, especially as it contextualises the swooning with other types of hysterical reaction, which is particularly vivid in the conventional island sickness scene (74).

As such, the weak and hysterical female castaway, who has somehow forgotten about her agency and empowerment as symbolised by the Amazonian bow and arrows, manages to survive not thanks to her own ingenuity and prowess but by following the advice of her predecessor on the island. It is telling that in the paradigmatic monarch-of-all-I-survey scene, which takes place shortly after Unca is left on the island, the heroine does not marvel at the environs nor fantasise about her dominance, but instead notices remnants of a hermit's dwelling, "the ruins of a building" (66), which imply, in a sense, that the land has already been taken. Inside, Unca discovers a manuscript book written by the hermit conveying advice: "How you may subsist, you may learn from the history of my life" (67). Fulfilling, as it were, Philip Quarll's prophecies about an inheritor to "his" island, Unca Eliza is situated here in a paternal line of succession, contrasting the maternal line of her Amazonian aunt, and her survival is accordingly made possible by "doing as she is told".

The shift from the narrative of survival to the narrative of colonisation takes place when Unca's stereotypically weak female constitution characterises her account of symbolic death and rebirth:

> I sat dissolved in sighs and tears, and indulged my melancholy, till the night drew on, when I laid me down, but not to rest; and so greatly was my mind afflicted, that it brought on a violent fever, attended with a delirium. I raved, I cried, I laughed by turns. I soon became so weak, that I was scarce able to crawl from my bed to get some water [...]. (74)

---

26   Ildiko Csengei, *Sympathy, Sensibility and the Literature of Feeling in the Eighteenth Century* (Houndmills: Palgrave Macmillan, 2011), p. 143.

27   Csengei, *Sympathy, Sensibility and the Literature of Feeling in the Eighteenth Century*, p. 142.

THE FEMALE AMERICAN (1767): A FAILED AMAZON 77

The description of Unca's fever is followed by a metaphorical bodily meta-morphosis that redefines her identity as a castaway. The female American is literally brought to the ground: she is forced to "crawl upon [her] hands and feet" to drink water; she "crawls upon the shore", "crawls" back to her cell, and "crawls" to find respite under a shade (74–76). Her symbolic death is followed by an allegory of baptism when she falls into a river and temporarily regains her strength, a cure completed when Unca helps herself to the dugs of a "she-goat asleep" (75). The castaway's revival, then, combines religious allegory with indications of "island infection", prompting a devolution into an animal state. But the hint of devolution is not indicative of "going native"; rather, by alluding to Ibn Tufayl's twelfth-century Arabic castaway tale *Hayy Ibn Yaqzan*,[28] which tells the story of an infant nourished by a gazelle and who in the course of his isolation develops an idea of God, the novel uses the death-rebirth pattern typical of the Robinsonade in general to indicate a shift from the story of sur-vival and isolation to a story of religious growth and Christianisation. Matthew Reilly, who considers *Hayy Ibn Yaqzan* to have been *The Female American*'s "most important influence", argues that this scene shows how Unca Eliza "does not share Crusoe's fear of the body" and develops a new "sensuous" self, aware of "the limitations to active agency" and appreciative of the "prereflective, hor-izontal engagement with the environment". This scene would thus represent the novel's idea of "movement from bodily experience towards a sense of being and belonging", reminiscent of the Arabic narrative.[29] This may well be the case, given the religious dimension of Unca's symbolic death, but in the latter section of the narrative the castaway's activities clearly go beyond a realisation of "Quaker spiritual values", whereby the heroine, rather than "imposing a pre-figured social, religious, and economic order on the landscape and people she meets, [...] immerses herself in her environment and unveils new prospects for becoming".[30] Unca does regain agency, but in exercising it she does exactly what her father figures, representative of "a prefigured social, religious, and economic order", would expect her to do.

---

28   The author of *The Female American* would have familiarised themselves with the 1708 English translation of Simon Ockley, titled *The Improvement of Human Reason: Exhibited in the Life of Hai Ebn Yokdhan*. For a study of its possible influence on Defoe, see Samar Attar, "Serving God or Mammon? Echoes from *Hayy Ibn Yaqzan* and *Sinbad the Sailor* in *Robinson Crusoe*", *Robinson Crusoe: Myths and Metamorphoses*, ed. Lieve Spaas and Brian Stimpson (Houndmills: Macmillan, 1996), pp. 78–97.

29   Matthew Reilly, "'No eye has seen, or ear heard': Arabic Sources for Quaker Subjectivity in Unca Eliza Winkfield's *The Female American*", *Eighteenth-Century Studies* 44.2 (2011): 262, 263.

30   Reilly, "No eye has seen, or ear heard", p. 278.

78   CHAPTER 4

First, she accounts for how her uncle finally took precedence over the aunt:

> [I]t was always my custom to imagine to myself that my uncle was speak-
> ing to me; this I thought, as it were, inspired me, and gave an energy to
> my words, strength to my arguments, and commanded my attention. I
> have sometimes indulged this reverie to such a degree that I have really
> imagined, at last, that my uncle was speaking to me. (77)

Having reasserted her identity as her uncle's disciple, rather than her aunt's
warrior – and indeed, the name "Unca" does not seem to be only accidentally
reminiscent of "uncle" – the castaway is finally confronted with her other father
figure, the old hermit, who – contrary to Unca's and the reader's expectations –
has not yet passed away. Thus reinstated in the patriarchal order of succession,
Unca begins her missionary work shortly after the hermit finally dies.

The castaway orchestrates her missionary work through two metamorphoses of her body. The first is related to how she literally incorporates, or allows
herself to be incorporated by the direct instrument of conquest and Christianisation, a monumental idol that she locates on the island:

> The image itself, of gold, greatly exceeded human size: it resembled a man
> clad in a long robe or vest; which reached quite down to the pedestal-
> stone or foundation on which it stood, and lay in folds upon it. This image
> was girt about the waist as with a girdle, and on each breast gathered to a
> point, fastened as it were, with a button; the neck and bosom quite bear
> like the manner of women; on the head was a curiously wrought crown,
> and between the two breasts an image of the sun carved in gold, as was all
> the rest of it. The right hand supported the figure of a new moon, and the
> left held a cluster of stars. On the back part of the idol was written in large
> Indian characters to this purpose, THE ORACLE OF THE SUN. I ascended
> the steps, and threw a stone at the image, and found it was hollow. (86)

While the feminine elements may be read as corresponding to Unca Eliza's
ensuing use of the idol, they principally indicate masculine power; this is later
confirmed when we learn that, typically, only male priests are permitted to
listen to the oracle. As such, it can be interpreted (as Ann Beebe suggests) as
a "phallic symbol",[31] not only given its vertical shape, but also its role as an
instrument of power over discourse. In becoming one with the idol to carry

---

31   Ann Beebe, "'I Sent Over These Adventures': Women in *The Female American* and *The
        Widow Ranter*", *Women's Studies* 45.7 (2016): 633.

THE FEMALE AMERICAN (1767): A FAILED AMAZON

out missionary work, Unca metaphorically re-enacts her reinstatement in the paternal line of her uncle and the hermit, her spiritual fathers:

> [The stairs] were very narrow and steep; which I soon found, led me up into the image of the sun. At last I got quite into the body of it, and my head within the head of it. There were holes through the mouth, eyes, nose, and ears of it, so that I could distinctly see all over the island before me, of which the height I was at gave me a great command. (88)

Unca's metaphorical transformation into an embodiment of patriarchal discourse tellingly alludes to, or perhaps corrects the monarch-of-all-I-survey moment that failed to offer any sense of empowerment at the beginning of the island narrative. Here, the female castaway is given "a great command" – yet not as an Amazon, but through incorporating masculine power. And as such, she hardly recognises herself: "I was almost stunned with the sound of my own voice" (88).

The second bodily metamorphosis takes place when the castaway (as oracle) has already subjugated the native people and obliged them to expect and obey a female religious leader who would continue their Christian education. Announced in this manner, Unca takes great care to appear as inspiring as possible, making use of the treasures she discovers in the subterranean rooms beneath the idol:

> When the expected morning came, I awoke by day-break, drest myself in white, and, over all, put on the high-priest's vestments [...]. These were a kind of cassock, or vest, formed of gold wire, or rather of small narrow plated gold, curiously folded, or twisted together, line net-work, which buttoned close with diamonds. Over this I put on, formed of the same materials, and in the same manner, a gown, sprinkled all over with precious stones, and here and there a large diamond. On my head I placed a crown of most exquisite make, richly beset with precious stones of various sizes and colours; one on the top particularly large, which emitted from all parts of it a light greater than that of either of my lamps. In my right hand I held a golden staff, or rod, with a small image of the sun on the top of it. On one of my fingers I wore the ring, and on each arm a rich bracelet, all which I found at the same time I discovered all these other things. (121)

While Unca's "mixed habit" in England was, in a sense, an internalised aspect of her hybrid identity, indispensably connected with her "tawny complexion" and with the bow and arrows, her masquerade in this scene more stridently demonstrates colonial appropriation, a stratagem which involves playing with the expectations of the indigenous people. Unca effectively attempts to carry out the imperial task imposed on her by her father figures, but she does so through an empowered playfulness with her dressed body, performed out of the home, in an adventurous manner. Unca does not remain faithful to her Amazonian origins, but she does find a space of empowerment within the imperial agenda; she may be a failed Amazon, but she becomes a successful female colonist. This idea has been taken up by Chloe Wigston Smith, who analyses Unca's dressed body as reflective of an imperialist fantasy of "colonial domestication", with a female protagonist who exercises her agency not through needlework but through a creative exploration and domestication of material otherness.[32] Unca's masquerade can also be read through the prism of Castle's arguments: the female American succeeds in creating a utopia of female sovereignty, but it is clearly not a society "unmarked by patriarchy".[33] When the locals want Unca as their queen, she is not interested: "I will not be your queen [...] I will come and live among you, and will be only your instructor" (123). A mere instructor, however clever in maintaining her position, Unca remains under the shadow of the father figures; in rejecting the offer to become a queen, she rejects the circular fulfilment of her destiny as an inheritor of her Amazon aunt, and opts for the linear progress of colonial rule.

The implicit presence of Uncle Winkfield behind the castaway's missionary work materialises in the final section of the novel, when Unca's cousin, whose advances she had mocked and rejected back at home, comes to her "rescue" having learned about her plight. The reappearance of the familiar in Unca's world momentarily reinstates the heroine in her role as an Amazon challenging the patriarchal order in a manner reminiscent of the pre-island section. She ridicules courtship and pretends not to hear her cousin's expressions of love while displaying her bodily difference, now with the help of the idol and the items she finds beneath it. She appears to the "rescuers" as a solar goddess, to the accompaniment of an Aeolian harp she has constructed: "The musick still sounding, I then stopped, holding my staff so that the image of the sun, on the top of it, prevented a full view of my face" (134). Unca's "extraordinary appearance" (134) and carefully staged performance together create an attempt to appropriate the possibilities granted by the "masculine" idol and to playfully reverse the power structure. That said, the empowering masquerade has its irreversible consequences, foreshadowed by cousin Winkfield's observation

---

32   Wigston Smith, "The Empire of Home", pp. 73–79.
33   Castle, *Masquerade and Civilisation*, p. 255.

THE FEMALE AMERICAN (1767): A FAILED AMAZON   81

that Unca's voice, emanating from the statue, was "monstrous" (135). The superstitious sailors want to have nothing to do with what they take to be a "she-devil [...] wrapt in gold" (137), somehow connected with "a monster as tall as the moon" (138):

> the sailors it seems heard the musick from the statue, as the wind blew directly off from the island; this together with my tawny complexion, and strange dress, so terrified them, that they [...] would come no nearer. (137)

As long as Unca's display of bodily difference was confined within the bounds of the familiar at home, she could be treated "in a degree little inferior to that of a princess" (58) and her hybrid constitution was an attractive "oddity" (58), despite the tinge of the Amazonian disposition she revealed. In the wider world, difference, especially female, turns out to be dangerous, and Unca's colonial masquerade accordingly invites corrective chastisement: there is no way that a "she-devil" can be taken back to England, so she remains a colonial missionary in the New World, and since cousin Winkfield is adamant that his "rescue" operation must be successful, she is finally talked into marriage:

> I had now the great pleasure of once more enjoying all the ordinances of the church, and the constant company of a religious and sensible companion, to whom, through his constant importunity, I was at last obliged to give my hand. (148)

In a sense, in becoming one body with her husband, tellingly captured through the use of "we" instead of "I" towards the end of the narrative, Unca re-incorporates the idol – a phallic symbol standing for masculine discursive rule – in a manner that somehow fulfils her earlier anxieties: when she intended to use the idol in her missionary work, she faced the dangerous threat of being entombed alive in it when an earthquake struck and she was still inside the statue. She hurt herself trying to escape:

> I groped my way as well as I could to the stairs, which led up to the trapdoor, which, having reached, I endeavoured to unbolt; but as the bolts were large and very rusty, they gave me a great deal of trouble and much pain, forced the skin off my hands, and made them very sore and bloody. (96)

The warning, realised through bodily pain, materialises at the end of the novel, when she is metaphorically buried alive through her incorporation of the male order. The idol survived the earthquake, and Unca was able to leave it, but now that she is one with cousin Winkfield, part of the "we" in the narrative, the inescapability of her position is rendered through what the couple decide to do with the idol: "we first determined to go upon my island, to collect all the gold treasure there, to blow up the subterraneous passage, and the statue, that the Indians might never be tempted to their former idolatry" (162). The destruction of the idol is thus invested with allegorical significance, reflective of the castaway's own disposition. This scene strongly resembles the parallel scenario in Defoe's *Farther Adventures*. While in Defoe's narrative the risky burning of the Tartarian idol highlighted Crusoe's susceptibility to the uncontrollable actions of the passions,[34] the blowing up of the statue in *The Female American* tells a different story: it represents Unca's burial alive in the incorporated masculine order. Once an Amazon and playful masquerader, she is now safely deposited within the frames of imperial, male-controlled missionary work in the New World, curating the legacy of her father figures, while the uncle in England, ironically, may "generously" take care of the earthly wealth she inherited from her biological father (161).

The Female American sacrifices its Amazon at the altar of the founding myth of America: unlike in *Peter Wilkins*, the myth of origin here does not support the hero myth; conversely, it requires an abandonment of (Amazonian and matrilineal) heroism for the sake of fatherly collectivism. Unca's colony, established through a peaceful evangelical mission, is a metaphor for subjugated America, and the biracial heroine becomes its embodiment. As Wigston Smith points out, Unca's "mixed habit" is reminiscent of visual allegories of the "new" continent in the period – especially those combining "domesticated" indigenous objects (dress, bow and arrow) with Europeanness (classical iconography).[35] The iconographic form of these allegories was codified by Cesare Ripa's influential *Iconologia*, first published in 1593 but regularly reprinted. Unca's allegorisation in *The Female American* becomes manifest when her early character sketch is juxtaposed with the later account of how she revealed herself before the native people: the indicators of racial and cultural difference (tawny skin, dress) and mentions of her bow skills, constructing a character of flesh and bone, give way to a simulacrum. Unca becomes an idea that is largely disembodied in as much as her authentic bodily difference

---

34 See Maximillian E. Novak, "Crusoe's Encounters with the World and the Problem of Justice in *The Farther Adventures*", Robinson Crusoe *after 300 Years*, ed. Andreas K. E. Mueller and Glynis Ridley (Lewisburg: Bucknell University Press, 2021), p. 178.

35 Wigston Smith, "The Empire of Home", pp. 75–77.

transforms into a masquerade outfit, with the bow – notably – playing merely a decorative function.

In sum, while in comparison with the other examples studied in this book Unca's hybrid, Amazonian body seems to offer the most subversive potential to challenge the ideal of imperial masculinity, in the end the protagonist is little more than a failed Amazon, who preserves her bodily and cultural difference and at times displays it, but who is unable to empower herself through it beyond theatrical stratagems that cohere with the larger picture of cultural dominance. As Brown has noted, the myth of the Amazon in literature often has a spectral dimension, being a shadowy presence, not necessarily realised: "Amazons haunt the frontiers of the representation of women at various levels and in various modes of discourse".[36] This is the case for Unca: in *The Female American*, her physical hybridity eventually remains little more than a textualised emblem of a peaceful interracial and intercultural encounter, part of a colonial fantasy into which the narrative transforms. Nevertheless, taking up Brown's idea of haunting presence, the castaway Amazon remains a powerful concept subverting the conventional distribution of roles in eighteenth-century Robinsonades. This concept is given an alluring embodiment in *The Female American*, and while Unca eventually fails as an Amazon, perhaps in part due to the formal and ideological requirements of the eighteenth-century castaway narrative as a genre, she stands out as the most memorable "female Crusoe" in the period, a point of reference for more recent revisions of the *Crusoe* story, such as Coetzee's *Foe*, offering, as we shall see, a more consistent application of the Amazonian myth.

---

36 Brown, *Ends of Empire*, 144.

Coda: Castaway Bodies in the Counter-Canonical Robinsonade

Elaborating on Daniel Defoe's ambiguous representation of Crusoe, the three Robinsonades discussed so far offer ideologically conflicted and aesthetically complex approaches to the castaway's bodily change; each is endowed with the hint of a progressive, counter-canonical message, but at the same time each is invariably attracted to the ideal of imperial masculinity. As such, the imagery of the body in *The English Hermit, Peter Wilkins* and *The Female American* is characterised by a double-voicedness that juxtaposes the standard colonial agenda of the eighteenth-century Robinsonade with subversive qualities that go beyond the genre's imperialist ideologies. In doing so, these novels rewrite myths of bodily metamorphosis, suggesting that the island may become a space of evolution, rather than devolution, and thus alleviating the fear of "going native" or "island infection" that typically characterised castaway narratives after *Robinson Crusoe*. They feature Bakhtinian "grotesque" bodies, in as much as they symbolise the castaways' porousness, or openness, to influence, and underline the ways in which they negotiate the "classical" ideal of the closed body – protected and disciplined.

The rationale for what follows works on the assumption that through *placing* these three eighteenth-century Robinsonades alongside three counter-canonical examples from the twentieth and twenty-first centuries, it will be possible to highlight what was non-standard, possibly subversive and ahead of its time in *The English Hermit, Peter Wilkins* and *The Female American*. In turn, it allows us to read these more recent examples – Tournier's *Friday*, Tokarczuk's "The Island" and Coetzee's *Foe* – in a historical context that establishes continuity within the Robinsonade tradition and its preoccupation with the castaway's body. In closing this book with a reading of contemporary variants of the myths discussed in it, I am inadvertently following in the footsteps of Ian Watt, who undertook a similar transhistorical comparison in the Coda to his *Myths of Modern Individualism: Faust, Don Quixote, Don Juan, Robinson Crusoe* (1996). While my readings are not, and have not been, overtly Wattian, and the parallel structure is more of a coincidence than a planned tribute, the structural analogy appears to be a natural consequence of a myth-critical perspective: regardless of the historical period prioritised and the material selected, the analysis would remain somehow incomplete without a leap in time towards the present and a glance, however cursory, at how the relevant myths have been reworked in a more immediate temporal context.

© KONINKLIJKE BRILL NV, LEIDEN, 2024 | DOI:10.1163/9789004692916_007

CODA: CASTAWAY BODIES IN THE COUNTER-CANONICAL ROBINSONADE 85

1   The Elemental Body in Michel Tournier's *Friday*

Michel Tournier's *Friday, or The Other Island*, originally published as *Vendredi, ou les Limbes du Pacifique* in 1967 (the English translation by Norman Denny appeared in 1969), is now a classic counter-Robinsonade that writes against the nineteenth-century imperial variant on several levels. Arguably, the three most significant aspects of this reinterpretation are Robinson's approach to the environment, his relationship with Friday, and the role of the symbolic order, that is, discursive power strategies exercised through the language of law. Rejecting the colonial heritage of the genre, Tournier ensures that his castaway fails to subjugate the land, and that his Friday is not "willing love learn" and has little respect for Robinson's grotesquely extensive ordering of their social life through written rules; unsurprisingly, Friday succeeds in escaping from the island at the first opportunity. Straightforward in its counter-canonical agenda, Tournier's novel is also, and perhaps above all, about the castaway's bodily metamorphosis. Elaborating on the Robinsonade's dialectic of devolution and growth, *Friday* is a narrative of change through a symbolic death of the body and its subsequent rebirth from the depths of the island. In this, Tournier's novel offers a more consistently ecological variant of the myth of the New Adam: what was foreshadowed in *The English Hermit* could now play out powerfully in the context of the 1960s and the rise of environmental awareness. The work of Rachel Carson in the 1950s and 1960s, including her milestone *Silent Spring* of 1962, the activism of James F. Phillips and others, and finally the first Earth Day held on 22 April 1970 provide some of the major elements constructing the broader panorama of ecological thought in the 1960s, and Tournier's immediate background when writing *Friday*.

The bodily change in the novel is already marked at the beginning of the narrative, when the castaway's failure to drag a boat he has built to the water almost drives him "out of his senses".[1] Realising his limitations and the likely future that awaits him, Robinson despairs and finds consolation in total inertia, and submerges himself naked in the swamp. Watt interprets this scene in the context of the Robinsonade's discourse of devolution, writing that the castaway "laps[es] into an animal condition" and, "like the peccaries or wild pigs, immerses himself totally, apart from eyes, nose, and mouth, in the muddy slime".[2] But, in arguing this, Watt ignores what preceded the

---

1   Michel Tournier, *Friday*, trans. Norman Denny (1967; Baltimore: Johns Hopkins University Press, 1997), p. 39. Further references to *Friday* will be parenthetical.

2   Ian Watt, *Myths of Modern Individualism: Faust, Don Quixote, Don Juan, Robinson Crusoe* (Cambridge: Cambridge University Press, 1996), p. 257.

scene: the castaway's gradual appreciation of his naked body and his growing awareness of the arbitrariness of the conventions of dress. When work on the boat is interrupted by the rain, he experiences a quasi-epiphanic moment of self-recognition:

> he was soon obliged to strip off his clothes, whose sodden weight hampered his movements. [...] he stood for a moment watching the tepid water flow over his body, carrying away its accretions of earth and dirt in little muddy balls. His ginger body hair, now plastered down and glistening, was patterned by the rain's lines of force, which accentuated its animal nature. (32)

Robinson does indeed recognise an affinity between himself and the animal state, and even chooses an alter ego – "a golden seal" – but this has nothing to do with the devolution into the beastly state that Defoe's Crusoe fears and Verne's Ayerton exemplifies. Instead, the appreciation of his naked body that Tournier's Robinson experiences, and his recognition of how it merges with the elements of earth and water, brings to his mind childhood memories; rather than "going native", the castaway, very much like Longueville's hermit, transforms back into a "natural" state – here, as the innocent child of both his human mother and Mother Earth. The swamp scene represents the symbolic retreat of a crying child into Mother Nature's comforting womb.

Tournier also establishes a dialectic between a "natural", naked body, at times helpless and idle in the depths of the earthly womb, with the disciplined body, shaped through labour:

> The *Escape* [i.e., the boat] was eventually completed, but the long tale of its building was inscribed forever on Robinson's flesh. Cuts, burns, scars, bruises, and calluses bore witness to the dogged battle he had waged for so long to produce this uncouth but sturdy-looking boat. There was no builder's time sheet, but his own body was record enough. (37)

So, while Robinson's union with Mother Earth in the swamp is indeed similar to the activities of the island's "peccaries or wild pigs", the castaway's body, hurt through disciplining labour, becomes rejuvenated when immersed in comforting and intoxicating idleness in the swamp: "Here, in its warm coverlet of slime, his body lost all weight, while the toxic emanations of the stagnant water drugged his mind" (40). Robinson's inertia lies at the core of Tournier's counter-writing in *Friday*, a powerfully tangible response – in its multi-sensual representation – to the emblematic erect body of the imperial castaway, ready

CODA: CASTAWAY BODIES IN THE COUNTER-CANONICAL ROBINSONADE 87

for action, brandishing a rifle and perhaps ascending a hill to survey the land. Tournier's appreciation of the idle body, also projected through contrast to conceptually linked discipline and body damage (rather than muscular athleticism as we have seen in other Robinsonades), nods towards ecocritical re-evaluations of idleness and its ecologies when seen as the alternative to the ethics of hard work and its environmental consequences.

In narrating a positively valued (d)evolution, Tournier's novel echoes the mythical patterns of *The English Hermit*, recalling its reversion to a pre-"civilised" state through sensual discourse and indications of the castaway's harmonious coexistence with the environment. But *Friday*, like Longueville's novel, also shows how symbolic death and rebirth eventually bring the castaway close to embodying the ideal of imperial masculinity, initially undermined by how the two castaways embrace "island infection". To Quarll it meant starting to hunt, controlling the monkeys on the island, taking a servant, calling himself the "lord" of the island and considering issues of inheritance. In *Friday*, post-swamp Robinson almost becomes a parody of the coloniser with his excessively accumulative capitalism and gargantuan law system. That said, Tournier's Robinson gradually changes, and his exploration reveals that there is more to the island, called Speranza – the island of hope – than it being a space of conquest: it is also "a place more alive, warmer and more fraternal, which his mundane preoccupations had concealed from him" (90). Re-enacting his withdrawal into the swamp inertia, he takes moments of respite in a deep cavern beyond his habitation, which serves a double symbolic function as both descent into the motherly womb and penetration. Krzysztof Skonieczny has traced this trajectory of change in Tournier's Robinson, using the concept of "becoming-Earth" developed by the posthumanist critic Rosi Braidotti, and understood as "reconfiguring the relationship to our complex habitat, which we used to call 'nature'".[3] Adopting the metonymic pattern of the I-land, which is central to the Robinsonade in general, Tournier's protagonist admits in the journal he keeps that "Robinson is Speranza. He is conscious of himself only in the stir of myrtle leaves with the sun's rays breaking through, he knows himself only in the white crest of a wave running up the yellow sand" (93). This unity is strengthened through the lovemaking scenes between Robinson and the Island, their offspring taking the shape of white mandrakes.

Tournier's castaway finally abandons the colonial ideal when confronted with the waywardness of Friday, who has no regard for Robinson's legal system

---

3 Quoted after Krzysztof Skonieczny, "Robinson's Becoming-Earth in Michel Tournier's *Vendredi*", *Rewriting Crusoe: The Robinsonade across Languages, Cultures, and Media*, ed. Jakub Lipski (Lewisburg: Bucknell University Press, 2020), p. 122.

and who ruins the settlement when he sets the stocks of gunpowder on fire with his careless pipe-smoking. This prompts a change in the castaway, whose relationship with the environment becomes less exploitative and more harmonious. Another form of symbolic death in the narrative, after shipwreck and swamp inertia, the explosion resonates with Robinson's bodily constitution: "In his heart he had longed for something of this kind to happen. [...] A new Robinson was sloughing off his old skin, fully prepared to accept the decay of his cultivated island and [...] enter upon an unknown road" (180).

While Longueville's hermit eventually embraced the New Adam's role of subjugating the Earth, Tournier's Robinson, understanding the futility of colonial ventures, reconfigures the myth, drawing it closer to the ecological spirit of the 1960s. Robinson's merger with the environment becomes the core of Tournier's counter-writing, just as the ultimate surfacing of imperial undertones in *The English Hermit* corrected the novel's subversive aspects. Tournier's New Adam defines his bodily change as "elemental": "The patterns of thought I had inherited from my fellow man crumbled and vanished. I groped about me, seeking salvation in communion with the elements, having myself become elemental" (209). The author himself commented on this sequence of change; referring to Baruch Spinoza's three stages of knowledge as described in *Ethics*, Tournier explained that in the case of his Robinson, "First there's the pig wallow, then the administered island, and the solar life, which somewhat resemble Spinoza's three kinds of knowledge, which are passion, scientific knowledge, and direct intuition of essence".[4] This "intuition of essence" constitutes Robinson's "elemental" state – a condition of reunion with essence, or "becoming-Earth", as Skonieczny has it.

The novel closes with Robinson's solar apotheosis:

> A blade of fire seemed to penetrate his flesh, causing his whole being to tremble. [...] He drew a deep breath [...] and his chest swelled like a breastplate of brass. His feet were solidly planted on the rock, and his legs sturdy and unshakable as columns of stone. The glowing light clad him in an armor of unfading youth and set upon his head a helmet flawlessly polished and a visor with diamond eyes. At length the sun-god unfolded his whole rich crown of flaming hair with a clash of cymbals and a fanfare of trumpets [...]. (234–235)

---

4 Susan Petit, *Michel Tournier's Metaphysical Fictions* (Amsterdam and Philadelphia: John Benjamins, 1991), p. 180.

CODA: CASTAWAY BODIES IN THE COUNTER-CANONICAL ROBINSONADE   89

Beyond its function within the internal logic of Tournier's novel, this bodily metamorphosis inadvertently alludes, in a corrective manner, to representations of castaways as colonial God-like father figures, as discussed by Weaver-Hightower. As we saw, this also provided the framework for Quarll's seemingly supernatural transformation; but the "elemental" change of Longueville's character, indicated by the cyclical rhythm of nature imprinted on his body, was eventually abandoned for civilisational linearity. Tournier fully realises the potential that was signalled in *The English Hermit*: the apotheosis depends on the castaway's communion with, rather than conquest of, the island, and is symbolised by an Ovidian bodily metamorphosis whereby the two entities become inseparable.

2   Conquering the Body in Olga Tokarczuk's "The Island"

Olga Tokarczuk's short story "Wyspa" ("The Island"), yet to be translated from Polish into English, was first published in the author's collection of short stories *Gra na wielu bębenkach* (*Playing on Many Drums*) in 2001. It was subsequently republished in 2018 in a modest volume of two stories, the other being "Profesor Andrews w Warszawie" ("Professor Andrews goes to Warsaw"), also originally in the 2001 collection, which plays with the convention of the urban Robinsonade, whereby the isolated protagonist is metaphorically cast away in a city that alienates them. While both stories are thus thematically and generically linked, it is "The Island" that foregrounds the castaway's body, first by elaborating on how it blends with the environment, and then by featuring an androgynous metamorphosis that, in a manner typical of Tokarczuk, dissolves the binaries that tend to organise our thinking.

"The Island" is a seemingly conventional Robinsonade, framed by two key events: shipwreck and rescue. The action takes place in 1944, and the nameless male protagonist, travelling from Greece to Palestine, survives a missile attack on his ship and finds shelter on a desert island. After sustaining himself with water and seafood, the castaway encounters a boat with an infant. As there is no way for him to feed the little one, he "conquers" his own bodily limitations and manages to force his body to breastfeed the child. They both survive and leave the island on a boat.

While it would be possible to read "The Island" in the context of Tokarczuk's wider work and its reliance on "bizarre" aesthetics and the central roles of movement, change, difference or anomaly, this short story can successfully be placed within the Robinsonade tradition, and especially the potentially subversive micro-tradition delineated so far. After all, Tokarczuk's story is in essence a relatively straightforward counter-canonical narrative, establishing its points of divergence through a skilful use of allusion, not only to Defoe's *Crusoe* and the imperial Robinsonade,[5] but also, even if accidentally, to the "counter-canonical canon" which includes Tournier's *Friday* and J. M. Coetzee's *Foe*. She follows *Friday*'s ecocritical agenda and elaborates on *Foe*'s concern with power over discourse – "The Island" is a first-person narrative recorded on a Dictaphone and addressed to a nameless fiction-writer who now owns the recording.

The bodily metamorphosis narrated in the story re-enacts the androgynous myth, but whereas in *Peter Wilkins* the mythical narrative problematised issues of gender and race, and was eventually abandoned – or appropriated – for the sake of colonial discourse, "The Island" stages the climactic transformation as part of its wider concerns with circularity, as opposed to imperial linearity, and speculative realism: in the narrator's words, his story is concerned with "the boundaries of the real, [...] between what is and what may be".[6] Key to Tokarczuk's agenda is questioning the nineteenth-century Robinsonade's ideal of progress and civilisational change that was, among other things, symbolised by the monarch-of-all-I-survey scene. While her castaway manages to climb one of the island's hills to view the environs, it is emphasised that this was not the highest hill, and that he failed in attempting to ascend the "top of the island". Instead, he circles around the beach, and wanders in "delineating overlapping spirals" (53), rather than fully exploring the land with a civilisational agenda. The routine circular patrol of the island, instead of hard work and cultivating improvement, becomes a form of quasi-disciplinary strategy, a response to the Robinsonade's conventional disciplinary labour: "I had to go round the island, like in a dream; to get up in the morning and go on the patrol as if it had been my job" (53). The protagonist learns about the island through those circular movements and finally discovers remnants of an older civilisation, perhaps the ruined settlements of his castaway predecessor. These have been gradually overgrown by the island flora to create a post-civilisational, if not post-apocalyptic, landscape:

---

5   In her meta-literary collection of essays – *Czuły narrator* (*The Tender Narrator*) – Tokarczuk recalls her childhood fascination with the fictions of Jules Verne. Olga Tokarczuk, *Czuły narrator* (Kraków: Wydawnictwo Literackie, 2020), pp. 105–106.

6   Olga Tokarczuk, *Profesor Andrews w Warszawie. Wyspa* (Warszawa: Wydawnictwo Literackie, 2018), p. 29. Further references to "Wyspa" will be parenthetical. Translations of quotations from Tokarczuk's short story are my own.

CODA: CASTAWAY BODIES IN THE COUNTER-CANONICAL ROBINSONADE   91

> The once ordered vineyards displayed no regularity; the stunted vine bushes, previously arranged in perfect lines, were now in chaotic disarray, reminiscent of twisted sticks, withered for years. The terraced slopes by the sea had lost their clear-cut shape and now resembled natural forms; the walls of stone were overgrown with vegetation [...]. (54–55)

Tokarczuk follows in Tournier's footsteps, and indirectly in those of Longueville, in treating the island as a space generating a new life, whereby it is the castaway who is to be born anew rather than the island itself. Like the French author, she uses environmental imagery that is meant to suggest that this new life will involve communion with the surroundings, both incorporated by the castaway and imprinted on his body:

> I felt as if I had been locked in my own self; as if the "I", which I had so far considered as something finite and absolutely real, was for a while revealed in a true light – I was something that contained somebody else. I was a shell, a rind, and inside there was a new being that was asking for life; a young, immature, mucous being, not yet ready, still in the process of becoming, if that was at all possible. (38)

Whereas in *Peter Wilkins* the fantasy of androgynous hybridisation was depicted as a potentially beneficial step forward, in an evolutionary sense, Tokarczuk – in a manner similar to Tournier – reduces her castaway to a prenatal stage, or, quite literally, *ab ovo*, which obfuscates the boundaries between the human world and that of flora and fauna, as the new being is endowed with features belonging to animal eggs and the seeds of plants or trees. Rather than being a land to be conquered and transformed, the island takes the castaway back to a state of potentiality, whereby the Crusoe-figure, rather than his environment, is compelled to undergo change.

Again reminiscent of Longueville and Tournier, Tokarczuk's castaway narrates his island experience using the language of the senses, recounting the touch of the wind and the beach's sand, the taste of seafood and drinking water, the smell of the sea: "I have transformed into my senses", he claims (33). The environment then literally imprints itself on the body. After spending some time in rocky terrain by a waterfall, he observes how the mineral-rich water changes his body: "I noticed how the limestone water left a white sediment in my hair. I looked as if I had gone grey" (48). Indeed, as the castaway relates, he had "grown onto the island like a mushroom onto a tree bark" (52).

The conceptual identification of the island and the castaway central to "The Island" is immediately signalled by the cover picture created by Joanna

Concejo (Figure 14), which shows a humanoid face as an island. This is confirmed later in the narrative, when the castaway observes that the oval island is characterised by two breast-shaped hills: the castaway's conquest of his own body, which yields to his wish to breast-feed the discovered infant, is metonymic of the conventional conquest of the island space.

If the first stage of the castaway's metamorphosis is precipitated by his identification with the island, the climactic point of androgynous change is brought about by his confrontation with the Friday figure – in this case an orphaned child, desperately in need of mother's milk, searching for a nipple with his mouth. "I felt mild cramps in my chest, from the breasts to the abdomen, like in the final wave of orgasm. [...] It felt as if my body inside had been organising itself anew", the castaway reports, "our bodies, in a sense, were now grown together" (69). The child, we read, "has now conquered the whole island" (71); within the logic of the I-land identification, this means it has conquered the castaway and his body:

> I looked at my naked torso, hairy and dirty with sand. My nipples were swollen and reddened. When I touched one of them, a drop of milk appeared. The same happened with the other. [...] It was as if the body in its mysterious doings had remembered its other possibilities, other embodiments, sedated potentialities. (73)

The motif of "other possibilities, other embodiments" recurs in Tokarczuk's fiction, as she writes about bodily metamorphoses (for example, in *Tales of the Bizarre*) or represents "abnormalities" displayed in cabinets of curiosities (as in *Flights*). The "open" body, not normalised and/or subject to change, contrasts

FIGURE 14   Joanna Concejo, the cover image to Olga Tokarczuk's *Profesor Andrews w Warszawie. Wyspa*
© JOANNA CONCEJO

CODA: CASTAWAY BODIES IN THE COUNTER-CANONICAL ROBINSONADE 93

with what she labels the "waterproof, impregnated" body of the Vernean protagonist, "closed in a capsule of his Western identity".[7] She writes against the representations of Crusoe-figures closed in capsules, and offers instead a narrative of "sedated potentialities" – here activated through a story of androgynous change that corresponds to her views, articulated explicitly elsewhere, on human sexuality as a "continuum".[8]

Concluding his Dictaphone narrative, the nameless castaway addresses the listening writer and asks to have the story "written up in a specific manner" (76). It is unclear what this "specific manner" means, but the castaway, unlike Coetzee's Susan Barton, as we shall see, resigns himself to the writer's power, in a way resolving the fiction/truth binary, as if in line with Tokarczuk's own dogma that "Fiction is always a kind of truth".[9] The metafictional conclusion refers to the opening of the story, when the narrator directly asks for his story to be turned into fiction and placed in a "collection of stories, the most fantastic ones" (29). The idea, then, is that fiction tests the possibilities and potentialities of the world, including of the embodied self. In the final sentence of the story the narrator expresses a hope that what he experienced "was not an anomaly, but a miracle" (76). The notion of anomaly assumes deviation from a norm (but reasserts it nevertheless); a miracle, by contrast, is an event that violates the accepted order of things. To Tokarczuk and her nameless castaway it is fiction that resists norms and negotiates the order of things that we take for granted.

3 Re-reading the Amazonian Myth in J. M. Coetzee's *Foe*

One of the most recognisable and arguably the most successful counter-canonical novels of the twentieth century, J. M. Coetzee's *Foe* of 1986 has sometimes been considered "a founding novel in the tradition of postcolonial revision".[10] The choice of the source text to revise must have been an easy one, given Coetzee's rather straightforward understanding of the colonial message of Defoe's novel: "*Robinson Crusoe* is unabashed propaganda for the extension of British mercantile power in the New World and the establishment of new British colonies", writes Coetzee, adding that "It is not [Defoe's] best book" and

---

7   Tokarczuk, *Czuły narrator*, p. 31.
8   Tokarczuk, *Czuły narrator*, p. 17.
9   Olga Tokarczuk, "The Tender Narrator", trans. Jennifer Croft and Antonia Lloyd-Jones, NobelPrize.org, https://www.nobelprize.org/uploads/2019/12/tokarczuk-lecture-english-2 .pdf, p. 11.
10   Fallon, *Global Crusoe*, p. 95.

that it "suffers as a result of hasty composition and lack of revision".[11] Coetzee's assessment reveals some of the stock criticisms of the past, but it did not obstruct the creation of an intriguing and enduring literary relationship, manifested not only by *Foe* and Coetzee's literary essays, but also, memorably, by Coetzee's Nobel Prize acceptance speech, for which the writer adopted the persona of Robinson Crusoe to ponder the questions of authorship and literary character ontology in a manner somehow reminiscent of Defoe's method in the preface to *Serious Reflections*.[12]

Establishing its metafictional identity by numerous allusions to *Crusoe* – not to mention featuring Defoe himself (under the original surname of Foe) in the novelistic world – and by drawing attention to the writing, editing and publishing process, as a Robinsonade, *Foe* is primarily concerned with power over discourse and the role of fiction and fiction-writing within hierarchic, often discriminatory, systems of meaning. The core of the novel's counter-writing, then, lies in empowering figures that have typically been marginalised in the Robinsonade tradition: the Friday figure and the female castaway. The narrative is told from the perspective of Susan Barton, who had met Cruso (the castaway's name is spelt in this way to undermine the accuracy of Foe's version of events) on "his" island; the story she tells is that of a failed colonist who eventually died on the island. A London scribe, Mr Foe, receives the "original" manuscript from Barton and – as we might assume, on the grounds of extra-textual knowledge – publishes a completely different narrative. The novel closes with the famous scene of Friday's wordless "speech", that is, a "slow stream" issuing from Friday's mouth that strongly affects the receptive writer-narrator: "it beats against my eyelids, against the skin of my face".[13] While Friday's body is clearly a key aspect of the novel,[14] my focus here is the Amazonian body of Susan Barton, who recalls Unca Eliza not only on the grounds that they share a comparable narrative context but also because both struggle to establish their agency in patriarchal systems of discourse and meaning.

Susan Barton does not become an Amazonian castaway because she is capable of surviving on the island without external help; on the contrary, she relies

---

11 J. M. Coetzee, *Stranger Shores: Literary Essays, 1986–1999* (New York: Viking, 2001), pp. 20–21.

12 J. M. Coetzee, "Nobel Lecture", 2003, https://www.nobelprize.org/prizes/literature/2003/coetzee/lecture/.

13 J. M. Coetzee, *Foe* (London: Penguin Books, 1987), p. 157. Further references to *Foe* will be parenthetical.

14 See, for example, Roman Silvani, *Political Bodies and the Body Politic in J.M. Coetzee's Novels* (Zürich and Berlin: LIT Verlag, 2012), pp. 83–92; and Olfa Belgacem, *The Body, Desire and Storytelling in Novels by J.M. Coetzee* (London and New York: Routledge, 2018).

CODA: CASTAWAY BODIES IN THE COUNTER-CANONICAL ROBINSONADE   95

completely on Cruso's and Friday's help, if not hospitality. She may appear more daring in questioning her host and undermining his island "rules", but eventually she remains confined to her role as female dependant, for which she "rewards" Cruso with passivity when he takes advantage of her in a troubling scene of sexual violence. Her Amazonian identity, however, is partially signalled by her appearance, which displays elements of "island infection" and a gradual erosion of conventional femininity: "The petticoat I had swum ashore in was in tatters. My skin was as brown as an Indian's. [...] When Friday set food before me I took it with dirty fingers and bolted it like a dog" (35). Apart from drawing attention to the typical indications of island devolution, Barton relates how the castaway experience has compromised her gender signifiers: here the petticoat, and later, when she is rescued, her dressed body in general: "No doubt I made a strange sight in a dark coat, borrowed from the captain, over sailor's pantaloons and apeskin sandals" (45).

But what really makes Susan Barton an Amazon in the novel is how she forces herself upon male-dominated discourse, in a manner comparable to Unca Eliza's incorporation of the idol. But while Unca's metaphorical transformation into the phallic monument symbolises the eventual abandonment of the Amazonian ideal and the heroine's identification with the line of the uncle, Coetzee's Susan Barton "would rather be the author of [her] own story" (40). And, just as Unca fantasises that she literally becomes the idol, the instrument of discursive power, so Barton imagines an analogical, though different, transformation when occupying Mr Foe's apartment, as he goes into hiding to avoid imprisonment for debt:

> I sat at your bureau this morning [...] and took out a clean sheet of paper and dipped pen in ink – your pen, your ink, I know, but somehow the pen becomes mine while I write with it, as though growing out of my hand – and wrote at the head: "The Female Castaway. Being a True Account of a Year Spent on a Desert Island. With Many Strange Circumstances Never Hitherto Related." (66–67)

In both *The Female American* and *Foe* the castaway heroines reach for discursive power that is exerted through the use of phallic objects: the idol and the pen. When becoming one with the idol, Unca does carry out her own stratagem and exercises her agency, but at the level of discourse her empowerment is confined within the patriarchal framework within which she was educated by her uncle. Susan Barton, in contrast, does not want to become a mediator but an author, telling her own story. She realises the pen and ink are Foe's – "your pen, your ink" – but fantasises that the pen becomes hers, an incorporated part of her. Occupying the vacant idol, Unca assumed a colonial stratagem that redefined her own, potentially subversive narrative into an imperial narrative of which her uncle would clearly approve. Occupying Foe's empty apartment, Susan Barton appropriates the instruments of discursive power and starts writing her own narrative, "never hitherto related", unlike the repetitive story of colonial conquest through Christianisation told by Unca.

That said, Coetzee's Susan Barton only goes as far as the title and eventually remains unsuccessful, the assumption being that Foe goes on to publish the version of the story that we all know. But what characterises Susan, even as she grows to accept her limited influence on Foe, is her indomitability in ascertaining that she is "a substantial body", just as the "vision of the island" that she shares with the scribe is "like a substantial body" (53). If her "substantiality" cannot be reasserted through her own island story, Coetzee's metafictional agenda enables her to do so through adopting nonconformist female roles familiar from Defoe's *Moll Flanders* and *The Fortunate Mistress*. The latter in particular provides the narrative framework into which Coetzee's Susan is inscribed following the island section, when her Amazonian self comes to the fore as an embodiment of Roxana (her real name, it is hinted in Defoe's novel, is also Susan), whose shape-shifting prowess guarantees survival in dismal urban spaces and on the road, where an isolated woman, or – much worse – a woman living freely with one male stranger (Friday) and imposing herself on another (Foe), and who also rejects her own child, has little chance of leading a respectable life.[15] Susan's body changes in terms of dress (from widow's garb to male breeches and coat to "pass for a man" [93, 101–102]) and physicality (with her wrinkles, dirty face, loss of colour, and lank hair [98, 108, 125]). She looks like a "gipsy", or like a "whore", but claims that the life of a respectable woman does not interest her: "I could return in every respect to the life of a substantial body, the life you recommend. But such a life is abject. It is the life of a thing. A whore used by men is used as a substantial body" (125–126). The convoluted logic of this remark, whereby a substantial (and respectable) body is abject, being objectified, while "a whore" gains a different sort of substantiality, is resolved through Susan's earlier assertion that she prefers the label of "free woman" to "whore" (109).

---

15   Engaging readings of Defoe's *The Fortunate Mistress* in the context of the Amazon myth include: Brown, *Ends of Empire*, chap. 5 and Shawn Lisa Maurer, "'I wou'd be a Man-Woman': Roxana's Amazonian Threat to the Ideology of Marriage", *Texas Studies in Literature and Language* 46.3 (2004): 363–386. Coetzee opened his volume of *Late Essays* with an insightful reading of *The Fortunate Mistress*, focusing on sexuality, psychology and the form of fiction. J. M. Coetzee, *Late Essays, 2006–2017* (New York: Viking, 2017), pp. 1–11.

CODA: CASTAWAY BODIES IN THE COUNTER-CANONICAL ROBINSONADE 97

Susan exercises her Amazonian freedom when, having been sexually used by Foe, she proceeds to pay him back and "straddle him" in "the manner of the Muse when she visits her poets" (139). Sex becomes part of her struggle over discourse and meaning; her earlier change of appearance involved cross-dressing and incorporating the masculine, very much in line with the Amazonian myth of "manlike" women, so that now "She must do whatever lies in her power to *father* her offspring" (140), just as she wants "to be *father* to [her] story" (123, emphasis mine). Not willing to yield to Foe's dominance, she re-enacts the dictum of Defoe's Roxana: "seeing Liberty seem'd to be the Men's Property, I wou'd be a *Man-Woman*; for as I was born free, I wou'd die so".[16]

Unlike Unca Eliza, Susan does not incorporate the masculine order to mediate it: she aspires to "father" a new order. And Coetzee adds a tinge of optimism to the narrative of Amazonian change: Susan might not be successful in having her own story published, but she is successful, as a mother/father figure, in empowering Friday: "A woman may bear a child she does not want, and rear it without loving it, yet be ready to defend it with her life. Thus it has become, in a manner of speaking, between Friday and myself. I do not love him, but he is mine" (111). It is Friday's story that she "fathers" when, in the final part of the novel, it surfaces quite literally over her dead body, in "the home of Friday", "a place where bodies are their own signs" (157).

The three more recent examples discussed here do not fully explore the richness of the still developing tradition of counter-canonical Robinsonades. What they have shown, however, is a peculiar line of continuity, whereby the process of rewriting is not so much about writing against as about writing to redress, elaborate upon or complete. Indeed, as Ann Marie Fallon suggests, "More often than not, writers [of contemporary Robinsonades] use these alternative Crusoes to forge lines of affiliation and empathy, between the eighteenth century and our own time as well as between different regions and languages".[17] While the eventual drive towards cultural supremacy, imperial rule and gender essentialism in the eighteenth-century texts addressed here may deserve scorn from a present-day perspective, there are nevertheless grounds for readerly empathy, established by the ideological double-voicedness of these narratives. The castaway's body becomes a space where these conflicting voices are tested against each other, corroborating Jason Farr's observation that eighteenth-century fiction in general demonstrates "an elasticity of thought about what

---

16   Daniel Defoe, *Roxana: The Fortunate Mistress*, ed. John Mullan (Oxford: Oxford University Press, 1996), p. 171.

17   Fallon, "Anti-Crusoes, Alternative Crusoes", p. 207.

makes bodies appear and act as they do".[18] The specificity of the castaway's body as a discursive space lies in the generic demands imposed upon it: it is by definition a metamorphosing body and – along with the island with which it establishes a metonymic relationship – a narrative and ideological axis of the Robinsonade. As this book has shown, the ideal of imperial masculinity, conventionally seen as central to the Robinsonade tradition, was already renegotiated in eighteenth-century examples of the genre, and the contemporary rejection of the colonial heritage of the Robinsonade and its ideological shift can be understood, in a Bakhtinian manner, as "contemporisation" rather than negation. This is how genres work, writes Bakhtin, by "constant renewal" in changing circumstances, but a renewal that never discards "the archaic elements preserved in a genre".[19] While the subversive undertones of the eighteenth-century texts discussed in this book could not play out entirely in their own contexts, they have become a foundation for the progressive turn in the contemporary Robinsonade, at the core of which is the metamorphosing body of the castaway that re-enacts mythical patterns of change.

---

18   Jason S. Farr, *Novel Bodies: Disability and Sexuality in the Eighteenth Century* (Lewisburg: Bucknell University Press, 2019), p. 1.

19   Bakhtin, *Problems of Dostoevsky's Poetics*, p. 106.

Bibliography

Abbé, Emelia "Collecting and Collected: Native American Subjectivity and Transatlantic Transactions in *The Female American*". *Early American Literature* 54. 1 (2019): 37–67.

Attar, Samar. "Serving God or Mammon? Echoes from *Hayy Ibn Yaqzan* and *Sinbad the Sailor* in *Robinson Crusoe*". *Robinson Crusoe: Myths and Metamorphoses*, ed. Lieve Spaas and Brian Stimpson. Houndmills: Macmillan, 1996, pp. 78–97.

Bakhtin, Mikhail. *Problems of Dostoevsky's Poetics*, ed. and trans. Caryl Emerson. Minneapolis: University of Minnesota Press, 1984.

Baines, Paul. "'Able Mechanick': *The Life and Adventures of Peter Wilkins* and the Eighteenth-Century Fantastic Voyage". *Anticipations: Essays on Early Science Fiction and Its Precursors*, ed. David Seed. Syracuse: Syracuse University Press, 1995, pp. 1–25.

Bannet, Eve Tavor. *Transatlantic Stories and the History of Reading, 1720–1810*. Cambridge: Cambridge University Press, 2011.

Beebe, Ann. "'I Sent Over These Adventures': Women in *The Female American* and *The Widow Ranter*". *Women's Studies* 45.7 (2016): 624–637.

Belgacem, Olfa. *The Body, Desire and Storytelling in Novels by J.M. Coetzee*. London and New York: Routledge, 2018.

Benedict, Barbara M. *Curiosity: A Cultural History of Early Modern Inquiry*. Chicago and London: The University of Chicago Press, 2001.

Bentley, Christopher. "Introduction". *The Life and Adventures of Peter Wilkins*, by Robert Paltock, ed. Christopher Bentley. London: Oxford University Press, 1973, pp. IX–XVIII.

Bhabha, Homi K. *The Location of Culture*. London and New York: Routledge, 1994.

Białas, Zbigniew. *The Body Wall: Somatics of Travelling and Discursive Practices*. Frankfurt am Main: Peter Lang, 2006.

Blaim, Artur. *The Adventurous Parable: Defoe's Robinson Crusoe*. Gdańsk: Wydawnictwo Gdańskie, 1994.

Blaim, Artur. *Robinson Crusoe and His Doubles: The English Robinsonade of the Eighteenth Century*. Frankfurt am Main: Peter Lang, 2016.

Blewett, David. "Robinson Crusoe, Friday, and the Noble Savage: The Illustration of the Rescue of Friday Scene in the Eighteenth Century". *Man and Nature / L'homme et la nature* 5 (1986): 29–49. https://doi.org/10.7202/1011850ar.

Blewett, David. "The Iconic Crusoe: Illustrations and Images of *Robinson Crusoe*." *The Cambridge Companion to "Robinson Crusoe"*, ed. John Richetti. Cambridge: Cambridge University Press, 2018, pp. 159–90.

Blewett, David. *The Illustration of Robinson Crusoe, 1719–1920*. Gerrards Cross: Colin Smythe, 1995.

Bohls, Elizabeth. "Age of Peregrination: Travel Writing and the Eighteenth-Century Novel". *A Companion to the Eighteenth-Century English Novel and Culture*, ed. Paula R. Backscheider and Catherine Ingrassia. Oxford: Blackwell, 2009, pp. 97–116.

Bowen, Scarlett. "Via Media: Transatlantic Anglicanism in *The Female American*". *The Eighteenth Century* 53.2 (2012): 189–207.

Bray, Libba. *Beauty Queens*. Crows Nest: Allen & Unwin, 2011.

Bristow, Joseph. *Empire Boys: Adventures in a Man's World*. London: HarperCollins Academic, 1991.

Brown, Laura. *Ends of Empire: Women and Ideology in Early Eighteenth-Century English Literature*. Ithaca, NY, and London: Cornell University Press, 1993.

Burnham, Michelle, and James Freitas. "A Note on the Text". *The Female American*, ed. Michelle Burnham and James Freitas. 2nd ed. Peterborough: Broadview editions, 2014, pp. 39–40.

Carey, Daniel. "Reading Contrapuntally: *Robinson Crusoe*, Slavery, and Postcolonial Theory". *Postcolonial Enlightenment*, ed. Daniel Carey and Lynn Festa. Oxford: Oxford University Press, 2009, pp. 105–136.

Castle, Terry. *Masquerade and Civilisation: The Carnivalesque in Eighteenth-Century English Culture and Fiction*. Stanford: Stanford University Press, 1986.

Chamberlain, Andrew T. "Morbid Osteology: Evidence for Autopsies, Dissection and Surgical Training from the Newcastle Infirmary Burial Ground (1753–1845)". *Anatomical Dissection in Enlightenment England and Beyond: Autopsy, Pathology and Display*, ed. Piers Mitchell. Farnham: Ashgate, 2012, pp. 11–22.

Coetzee, J. M. *Foe*. London: Penguin Books, 1987.

Coetzee, J. M. *Stranger Shores: Literary Essays, 1986–1999*. New York: Viking, 2001.

Coetzee, J. M. "Nobel Lecture", 2003, https://www.nobelprize.org/prizes/literature /2003/coetzee/lecture/.

Coetzee, J. M. *Late Essays, 2006–2017*. New York: Viking, 2017.

Collins-Frohlich, Jesslyn, and Denise Mary MacNeil. "Introduction". *Women's Studies* 45.7 (2016): 611–612.

Cook, Daniel. "Coda: Rewriting the Robinsonade". *Rewriting Crusoe: The Robinsonade across Languages, Cultures, and Media*, ed. Jakub Lipski. Lewisburg: Bucknell University Press, 2021, pp. 165–174.

Coupe, Laurence. *Myth*. London and New York: Routledge, 2009.

Crook, Nora. "Peter Wilkins: A Romantic Cult Book". *Reviewing Romanticism*, ed. Philip W. Martin and Robin Jarvis. London: Macmillan, 1992, pp. 86–98.

Csengei, Ildiko. *Sympathy, Sensibility and the Literature of Feeling in the Eighteenth Century*. Houndmills: Palgrave Macmillan, 2011.

Defoe, Daniel. *The True and Genuine Account of the Life and Actions of the Late Jonathan Wild. Jonathan Wild*, by Henry Fielding, ed. David Nokes. London: Penguin Books, 1986, pp. 221–257.

BIBLIOGRAPHY

Defoe, Daniel. *Roxana: The Fortunate Mistress*, ed. John Mullan. Oxford: Oxford University Press, 1996.

Defoe, Daniel. *The Strange Surprizing Adventures of Robinson Crusoe*, ed. Maximillian E. Novak, Irving N. Rothman, and Manuel Schonhorn. Lewisburg: Bucknell University Press, 2020.

Defoe, Daniel. *The Farther Adventures of Robinson Crusoe*, ed. Maximillian E. Novak, Irving N. Rothman, and Manuel Schonhorn. Lewisburg: Bucknell University Press, 2022.

Deleuze, Gilles. "Desert Islands". *Desert Islands and Other Texts 1953–1974*, ed. David Lapoujade, trans. Michael Taormina. Los Angeles: Semiotext(e), 2004, pp. 9–14.

Dibdin, Charles. *The Professional Life of Mr. C. Dibdin*. Vol. 3. London: Published by the Author.

Ellis, Markman. "Novel and Empire". *The Oxford Handbook of the Eighteenth-Century Novel*, ed. J.A. Downie. Oxford: Oxford University Press, 2016, pp. 489–504.

Fallon, Ann Marie. *Global Crusoes: Comparative Literature, Postcolonial Theory, and Transnational Aesthetics*. Farnham: Ashgate, 2011.

Fallon, Ann Marie. "Anti-Crusoes, Alternative Crusoes: Revisions of the Island Story in the Twentieth Century". *The Cambridge Companion to "Robinson Crusoe"*, ed. John Richetti. Cambridge: Cambridge University Press, 2018, pp. 207–220.

Farr, Jason S. *Novel Bodies: Disability and Sexuality in the Eighteenth Century*. Lewisburg: Bucknell University Press, 2019.

Fausett, David. *Images of the Antipodes in the Eighteenth Century: A Study in Stereotyping*. Amsterdam and Atlanta: Rodopi, 1995.

Folkenflik, Robert. "The Rise of the Illustrated English Novel to 1832". *The Oxford Handbook of the Eighteenth-Century Novel*, ed. J. A. Downie. Oxford: Oxford University Press, 2016, pp. 308–336.

Foucault, Michel. "Of Other Spaces", trans. Jay Miskowiec. *Diacritics* 16.1 (1986): 22–27.

Genette, Gérard. *Paratexts: Thresholds of Interpretation*, trans. J.E. Lewin. Cambridge: Cambridge University Press, 1997.

Goss, Erin M. *Revealing Bodies: Anatomy, Allegory, and the Grounds of Knowledge in the Long Eighteenth Century*. Lewisburg: Bucknell University Press, 2013.

Gove, Philip Babcock. *The Imaginary Voyage in Prose Fiction: A History of Its Criticism and a Guide for Its Study*. New York: Columbia University Press, 1941.

Green, Martin. *Dreams of Adventure, Deeds of Empire*. New York: Basic Books, 1979.

Hagglund, Elizabeth, and Jonathan Laidlow. "'A Man might find every thing in your Country': Improvement, Patriarchy, and Gender in Robert Paltock's *The Life and Adventures of Peter Wilkins*". *Gender and Utopia in the Eighteenth Century: Essays in English and French Utopian Writing*, ed. Nicole Pohl and Brenda Tooley. Burlington: Ashgate, 2007, pp. 133–146.

Hicks, Amy. "Romance, the Robinsonade, and the Cultivation of Adolescent Female Desire in Libba Bray's *Beauty Queens*". *Didactics and the Modern Robinsonade*, ed. Ian Kinane. Liverpool: Liverpool University Press, 2019, pp. 185–202.

Hobbes, Thomas. *The Elements of Law: Natural and Politic*, ed. Ferdinand Tönnies. Cambridge: Cambridge University Press, 1928.

Hulme, Peter. *Colonial Encounters: Europe and the Native Caribbean, 1492–1797*. London and New York: Methuen, 1986.

Houlihan Flynn, Carolyn. *The Body in Swift and Defoe*. Cambridge: Cambridge University Press, 1990.

Ibn Tufayl, *The Improvement of Human Reason: Exhibited in the Life of Hai Ebn Yokdhan*, trans. Simon Ockley. London: Edmund Powell, 1708.

Iwanisziw, Susan B. "Intermarriage in Late-Eighteenth-Century British Literature: Currents in Assimilation and Exclusion". *Eighteenth-Century Life* 31.2 (2007): 56–82.

Johns, Alessa. *Women's Utopias of the Eighteenth Century*. Urbana and Chicago: University of Illinois Press, 2003.

Joseph, Betty. "Re(playing) Crusoe/Pocahontas: Circum-Atlantic Stagings in *The Female American*", *Criticism* 42.3 (2000): 317–335.

Joyce, James. "Daniel Defoe". *Robinson Crusoe*, by Daniel Defoe, ed. Michael Shinagel. New York and London: Norton, 1994, pp. 320–323.

Jung, Sandro. "Amplifying Reading Experience: Illustrations to Longueville's *The English Hermit*, 1727–1799". *English Studies* 103.1 (2022): 42–62.

Kaul, Suvir. *Eighteenth-Century British Literature and Postcolonial Studies*. Edinburgh: Edinburgh University Press, 2009.

Kelly, Veronica, and Dorothea E. von Mücke, "Introduction: Body and Text in the Eighteenth Century". *Body and Text in the Eighteenth Century*, ed. Veronica Kelly and Dorothea E. von Mücke. Stanford: Stanford University Press, 1994, pp. 1–20.

Kinane, Ian. *Theorising Literary Islands: The Island Trope in Contemporary Robinsonade Narratives*. London and New York: Rowman & Littlefield International, 2017.

Kinane, Ian. "Introduction: The Robinsonade Genre and the Didactic Impulse: A Reassessment". *Didactics and the Modern Robinsonade*, ed. Ian Kinane. Liverpool: Liverpool University Press, 2019, pp. 1–52.

King, Sigrid. "Amazon". *Encyclopedia of Feminist Literary Theory*, ed. Elizabeth Kowaleski Wallace. London and New York: Routledge, 2009, pp. 16–17.

Kleinbaum, Abby Wettan. *The War against the Amazons*. New York: McGraw-Hill, 1983.

Korte, Barbara. *Body Language in Literature*. Toronto: University of Toronto Press, 1997.

Linker, Laura. *Dangerous Women, Libertine Epicures, and the Rise of Sensibility, 1670–1730*. Farnham: Ashgate, 2011.

Lipski, Jakub. *Painting the Novel: Pictorial Discourse in Eighteenth-Century English Fiction*. London and New York: Routledge, 2018.

BIBLIOGRAPHY

Lipski, Jakub. "Robert Paltock, *The Life and Adventures of Peter Wilkins* (1751)". *Handbook of the British Novel in the Long Eighteenth Century*, ed. Katrin Berndt and Alessa Johns. Berlin and Boston: De Gruyter, 2022, pp. 243–258.

Lipski, Jakub. "Three Mid-Eighteenth-Century Mashups: Hybridity and Conflicted Discourse in Robert Paltock's *Peter Wilkins* and Its Early Imitations". *1650–1850: Ideas, Aesthetics, and Inquiries in the Early Modern Era*. Vol. 28. Lewisburg: Bucknell University Press, 2023, pp. 119–139.

Longueville, Peter. *The English Hermit, or the Unparalell'd and Surprizing Adventures of one Philip Quarll*. London: Printed by J. Cluer and A. Campbell for T. Warner in Pater-Noster-Row, and B. Creake at the Bible in Jermyn-Street, St. James's, 1727.

Lupton, Christina. "Giving Power to the Medium: Recovering the 1750s". *The Eighteenth Century* 52.3/4 (2011): 289–302.

MacNeil, Denise Mary. "Empire and the Pan-Atlantic Self in *The Female American; or, The Adventures of Unca Eliza Winkfield*". *Women's Narratives of the Early Americas and the Formation of Empire*, ed. Mary McAleer Balkun and Susan C. Imbarrato. New York: Palgrave Macmillan, 2016, pp. 109–122.

Maurer, Shawn Lisa. "'I wou'd be a Man-Woman': Roxana's Amazonian Threat to the Ideology of Marriage". *Texas Studies in Literature and Language* 46.3 (2004): 363–386.

Marzec, Robert. *An Ecological and Postcolonial Study of Literature: From Daniel Defoe to Salman Rushdie*. New York: Palgrave, 2007.

McMaster, Juliet. *Reading the Body in the Eighteenth-Century Novel*. Houndmills: Palgrave Macmillan, 2004.

McMurran, Mary Helen. "Realism and the Unreal in *The Female American*". *The Eighteenth Century* 52.3/4 (2011): 323–342.

McQuigge, Alexis. "'That Person Shall be a Woman': Matriarchal Authority and the Fantasy of Female Power in *The Female American*". *Transatlantic Women Travelers, 1688–1843*, ed. Misty Krueger. Lewisburg: Bucknell University Press, 2021, pp. 131–143.

Meletinsky, Eleazar. *The Poetics of Myth*, trans. by Guy Lanoue and Alexandre Sadetsky. London and New York: Routledge, 1998.

Merchant, Peter. "Robert Paltock and the Refashioning of 'Inkle and Yarico'". *Eighteenth-Century Fiction* 9.1 (1996): 37–50.

Morris, Ralph. *A Narrative of the Life and Astonishing Adventures of John Daniel*. London: Printed for M. Cooper, 1751.

Munns, Jessica, and Penny Richards (eds.). *The Clothes that Wear Us: Essays on Dressing and Transgressing in Eighteenth-Century Culture*. Newark and London: University of Delaware Press, 1999.

Napier, Elizabeth R. *Falling into Matter: Problems of Embodiment in English Fiction from Defoe to Shelley*. Toronto: University of Toronto Press, 2012.

Novak, Maximillian E. "Picturing the Thing Itself, or Not: Defoe, Painting, Prose Fiction, and the Arts of Describing". *Eighteenth-Century Fiction* 9.1 (1996): 1–20.

Novak, Maximillian E. "Edenic Desires: *Robinson Crusoe*, the Robinsonade, and Utopian Forms". *Transformations, Ideology, and the Real in Defoe's* Robinson Crusoe *and Other Narratives: Finding the "Thing Itself"*. Newark: University of Delaware Press, 2015, pp. 111–127.

Novak, Maximillian E. *Transformations, Ideology, and the Real in Defoe's* Robinson Crusoe *and Other Narratives: Finding the "Thing Itself"*. Newark: University of Delaware Press, 2015.

Novak, Maximillian E. "Crusoe's Encounters with the World and the Problem of Justice in *The Farther Adventures*". Robinson Crusoe *after 300 Years*, ed. Andreas K. E. Mueller and Glynis Ridley. Lewisburg: Bucknell University Press, 2021, pp. 167–181.

O'Malley, Andrew. *Children's Literature, Popular Culture, and Robinson Crusoe*. Houndmills: Palgrave Macmillan, 2012.

O'Malley, Andrew. "The Progressive Pedagogies of the Modern Robinsonade". *Didactics and the Modern Robinsonade*, ed. Ian Kinane. Liverpool: Liverpool University Press, 2019, pp. XIII–XIV.

Ovid. *Metamorphoses*. London: Jacob Tonson, 1717.

Owen, C.M. *The Female Crusoe: Hybridity, Trade and the Eighteenth-Century Individual*. Amsterdam and New York: Rodopi, 2010.

Paltock, Robert. *The Life and Adventures of Peter Wilkins*, ed. Christopher Bentley. 1751. London: Oxford University Press, 1973.

Pearl, Jason H. "*Peter Wilkins* and the Eighteenth-Century Novel". *SEL Studies in English Literature 1500–1900* 57.3 (2017): 541–559.

Petit, Susan. *Michel Tournier's Metaphysical Fictions*. Amsterdam and Philadelphia: John Benjamins, 1991.

Pick, Daniel. *Faces of Degeneration: A European Disorder, c. 1848-c. 1914*. Cambridge: Cambridge University Press, 1989.

Prower, Siegbert. *Comparative Literary Studies: An Introduction*. London: Duckworth, 1973.

Rees, Christine. *Utopian Imagination and Eighteenth-Century Fiction*. London and New York: Routledge, 1996.

Reilly, Matthew. "'No eye has seen, or ear heard': Arabic Sources for Quaker Subjectivity in Unca Eliza Winkfield's *The Female American*". *Eighteenth-Century Studies* 44.2 (2011): 261–283.

Richetti, John, ed. *The Cambridge Companion to "Robinson Crusoe"*. Cambridge: Cambridge University Press, 2018.

Riquet, Johannes. *The Aesthetics of Island Space: Perception, Ideology, Geopoetics*. Oxford: Oxford University Press, 2019.

Rogers, Woodes. *A Cruising Voyage around the World*. 2nd ed. London: Andrew Bell, 1718.

BIBLIOGRAPHY

Rousseau, Jean-Jacques. *Emile, or On Education*. Ed. and trans. Christopher Kelly and Allan Bloom. Hanover, NH: University Press of New England, 2010.

Rønning, Anne Birgitte. "Female Robinsonades – A Bibliography". Universitetet i Oslo, 2011–2020. https://www2.hf.uio.no/tjenester/bibliografi/Robinsonades.

Sambrook, James. "Paltock, Robert". *Oxford Dictionary of National Biography*. https://www.oxforddnb.com/. Oxford: Oxford University Press, 2004 (30 July 2021).

Samson, Barney. *Desert Islands and the Liquid Modern*. Cham: Palgrave Macmillan, 2020.

Schmidgen, Wolfram. *Eighteenth-Century Fiction and the Law of Property*. Cambridge: Cambridge University Press, 2004.

Silvani, Roman. *Political Bodies and the Body Politic in J.M. Coetzee's Novels*. Zürich and Berlin: LIT Verlag, 2012.

Skonieczny, Krzysztof. "Robinson's Becoming-Earth in Michel Tournier's *Vendredi*". *Rewriting Crusoe: The Robinsonade across Languages, Cultures, and Media*, ed. Jakub Lipski. Lewisburg: Bucknell University Press, 2020, pp. 117–132.

Starr, G. A. *Defoe and Spiritual Autobiography*. Princeton: Princeton University Press, 1965.

Stimpson, Brian. "*Insulaire que tu es. Île–*: Valéry, the Robinson Crusoe of the Mind". *Robinson Crusoe: Myths and Metamorphoses*, ed. Lieve Spaas and Brian Stimpson. New York: St. Martin's Press, 1996, pp. 294–315.

Sutherland, A. Edward. *Mr. Robinson Crusoe*. United Artists.

Swenson, Rivka. "'Mushrooms, Capers, and Other Sorts of Pickles': Remaking Genre in Peter Longueville's *The Hermit* (1727)". *Rewriting Crusoe: The Robinsonade across Languages, Cultures, and Media*, ed. Jakub Lipski. Lewisburg: Bucknell University Press, 2020, pp. 9–22.

The Female American, ed. Michelle Burnham and James Freitas. 2nd ed. Peterborough: Broadview editions, 2014.

The Monthly Review. Vol. 4. London: Printed for R. Griffith, 1750.

Tokarczuk, Olga. *Profesor Andrews w Warszawie. Wyspa* [*Professor Andrews goes to Warsaw. The Island*]. Warszawa: Wydawnictwo Literackie, 2018.

Tokarczuk, Olga. "The Tender Narrator", trans. Jennifer Croft and Antonia Lloyd-Jones. NobelPrize.org., 2019, https://www.nobelprize.org/uploads/2019/12/tokarczuk-lecture-english-2.pdf.

Tokarczuk, Olga. *Czuły narrator* [*The Tender Narrator*]. Kraków: Wydawnictwo Literackie, 2020.

Tournier, Michel. *Friday*, trans. Norman Denny. 1967. Baltimore: Johns Hopkins University Press, 1997.

Uściński, Przemysław. "Castaways and Colonialism: Dislocating Cultural Encounter in The Female American (1767)". *Rewriting Crusoe: The Robinsonade across Languages, Cultures, and Media*, ed. Jakub Lipski. Lewisburg: Bucknell University Press, 2020, pp. 39–51.

Verne, Jules. *The Mysterious Island*. New York: C. Scribner's Sons, 1930.

Wahrman, Dror. *The Making of the Modern Self: Identity and Culture in Eighteenth-Century England*. New Haven: Yale University Press, 2004.

Watt, Ian. "Robinson Crusoe as a Myth". *Essays in Criticism* 1.2 (1951): 95–119.

Watt, Ian. *Myths of Modern Individualism: Faust, Don Quixote, Don Juan, Robinson Crusoe*. Cambridge: Cambridge University Press, 1996.

Watt, Ian. *The Rise of the Novel: Studies in Defoe, Richardson and Fielding*. 1957. Berkeley and Los Angeles: University of California Press, 2001.

Weaver-Hightower, Rebecca. *Empire Islands: Castaways, Cannibals, and Fantasies of Conquest*. Minneapolis: University of *Minnesota* Press, 2007.

Wheeler, Roxann. *The Complexion of Race: Categories of Difference in Eighteenth-Century British Culture*. Philadelphia: University of Pennsylvania Press, 2000.

Wheelwright, Julie. *Amazons and Military Maids: Women Who Dressed as Men in Pursuit of Life, Liberty and Happiness*. London: Pandora, 1989.

Wigston Smith, Chloe. "The Empire of Home: Global Domestic Objects and *The Female American* (1767)". *Journal for Eighteenth-Century Studies* 40.1 (2017): 67–87.

Index

Abbé, Emelia   70
Amazon, the   2, 4, 10, 11, 69, 71–76, 79–83, 93–97
Androgyne, the   2, 4, 9, 10, 49, 50, 54, 58, 63, 64, 89–93
Ansell, Charles   23, 25
Attar, Samar   77
Aubin, Penelope
 The Life of Charlotta Du Pont   68
 The Strange Adventures of the Count de Vinevil   68

Baines, Paul   49
Bakhtin, Mikhail   2, 31, 98
 polyphony   2, 4, 11, 23, 66
 the carnivalesque   31
Ballantyne, R. M.
 The Coral Island   1
Bannet, Eve Tavor   32
Beebe, Ann   78
Belgacem, Olfa   94
Benedict, Barbara M.   57
Bentley, Christopher   48
Bhabha, Homi K.   63
Białas, Zbigniew   5, 14, 21
Bible, the   9, 10, 37, 39, 44
Blaim, Artur   13, 32
Blewett, David   16, 22, 23, 25, 26
body, the
 allegory   5, 12, 13, 31, 39, 41, 82
 and the eighteenth-century novel   4, 5, 12, 37
 body politic   44, 45, 46
 discipline   5, 6, 7, 10, 15, 28, 33, 37, 46, 47, 55, 64, 84, 86, 87
 dress   16, 20–22, 30, 35, 38, 42, 63, 64, 73, 79, 80, 86, 95, 96
 metamorphosis   4, 5, 9–11, 19, 28, 31, 66, 77, 78–79, 84, 85, 88–90, 92, 98
 nakedness   7, 10, 21, 25, 28, 30, 35, 36, 39, 40, 42, 57, 85, 86, 92
 the classical body   31, 56, 66, 84
 the grotesque body   19, 21, 23, 31, 84
Bohls, Elizabeth   5

Boitard, Louis-Philippe   50–53, 56, 58, 60, 61, 66–67
Bowen, Scarlett   73
Braidotti, Rosi   87
Bray, Libba
 Beauty Queens   69
Bristow, Joseph   1, 2
Brown, Laura   71, 83, 96
Brown, Mather   23, 25
Burnham, Michelle   68, 70

Campe, J. H.
 Robinson der Jüngere   32
cannibalism   12, 14, 16, 46, 55
Carey, Daniel   1
Castle, Terry   71, 80
Chamberlain, Andrew T.   38
circularity   43, 44, 45, 46, 53, 80, 90
Clark, John   16, 17, 22, 23, 25, 28, 31
Coetzee, J. M.   94
 Foe   3, 83, 84, 90, 93–97
colonialism   1, 4, 6, 7, 9, 25, 30, 45, 62, 66, 76, 80, 82, 84, 87, 88, 98
Concejo, Joanna   92
Cook, Daniel   54
Coupe, Laurence   4
criminal biography   33, 35, 36, 38, 39
Crook, Nora   48
Cruikshank, George   25, 26
Crusoe Richard Davis   46
Csengei, Ildiko   76

Defoe, Daniel
 Account of Jonathan Wild   38
 and the body   12, 13, 14
 Moll Flanders   13, 96
 Robinson Crusoe   1, 2, 12–31, 32, 33, 48, 54, 57, 62, 63, 66, 68, 70, 86, 94
  ambiguity   2, 23, 30, 31
  and imperialism   1, 2, 16, 21, 25, 26, 30, 94
  and myth   4, 31
  character sketch   12, 16–23, 66, 84
  description   12, 13, 20, 23
  Friday   21, 22, 25, 30, 62, 63, 73
  illustrations   16–19, 22, 23–30

108 INDEX

Defoe, Daniel (*cont.*)
   Serious Reflections [...] of Robinson
      Crusoe 2, 94
   The Farther Adventures of Robinson
      Crusoe 2, 47, 58, 59, 82
   The Fortunate Mistress (Roxana) 13, 71,
      96, 97
degeneration 9, 15, 37, 60. *See* devolution
Deleuze, Gilles 6
devolution 7–9, 36, 47, 77, 84, 85–87, 95.
      See degeneration
Dibdin, Charles 72
   Hannah Hewit 72
dissection 38
dream 16, 41, 69

ecology 14, 35, 44, 46, 47, 64, 85, 87, 88
Eden 9, 10, 28–30, 33, 35, 37, 41, 45, 53, 56
Ellis, Markman 1
eroticism 41, 54, 56, 57
Evans, Ambrose
   The Adventures and Surprizing
      Deliverances of James Dubourdieu and
      His Wife 68

Fairbanks, Douglas 28, 29, 47
Fallon, Ann Marie 3, 93, 97
Farr, Jason S. 97, 98
father figure 21, 23, 35, 77, 78, 80, 82, 89, 97
Fausett, David 49, 58
femininity 10, 11, 62, 63, 68, 69, 72, 74, 76,
      78, 95
Férat, Jules 8
Flynn, Carolyn Houlihan 12
Folkenflik, Robert 22
Foucault, Michel 10, 43
Freitas, James 68, 70
Friday figure 25, 28, 35, 45, 85, 87, 92,
      94, 95, 96, 97
Frohlich, Jesslyn Collins 70

gender 10, 11, 50, 59, 62–64, 66, 69, 72, 73,
      90, 95, 97. *See* femininity, masculinity
Genette, Gérard 33
Gent, Thomas 23, 24
going native 14, 20, 42, 55, 77, 84, 86. *See*
      island: island infection
Goss, Erin M. 5
Gove, Philip Babcock 49

Green, Martin 26
Griset, Ernest 25

Hagglund, Elizabeth 50, 63
Hermaphrodite 10
Hicks, Amy 69
Hobbes, Thomas 44, 46
Hogarth, William
   A Rake's Progress 38
   The Four Stages of Cruelty 38–39
Hulme, Peter 62
hybridity 10, 11, 50, 54, 59–61, 62, 64, 68,
      72–74, 79, 81, 83, 91

Ibn Tufayl
   Hayy Ibn Yaqzan 77
idleness 86–87
imaginary voyage 32, 36, 43, 49
island
   as a configuration of self 5, 6, 84, 87,
      91–92, 98
   as a setting 10, 14, 33, 35, 36, 39, 43, 49,
      87, 90–91
   as heterotopia 9, 43, 45, 46, 71
   island infection 7–8, 15, 20, 37, 76–77,
      84, 87, 95. *See* going native
Iwanisziw, Susan B. 59

Joseph, Betty 73
Joyce, James 30–31
Jung, Sandro 32, 35

Kaul, Suvir 21
Kelly, Veronica 5
Kinane, Ian 2, 3, 6, 9–10, 35, 68, 69
King, Sigrid 71
Kleinbaum, Abby Wettan 71
Korte, Barbara 4–5, 12
Kristeva, Julia
   abjection 35, 96

labour 7, 10, 14, 15, 28, 37, 46, 54, 62, 63, 86,
      90
Laidlow, Jonathan 50, 63
linearity 43, 46, 53, 80, 89, 90
Linker, Laura 71
Longueville, Peter
   The English Hermit 2, 9, 32–47, 49, 54,
      55, 66, 69, 84, 85, 86, 87, 88, 89, 91

INDEX

Longueville, Peter (*cont.*)
    and imperialism 46, 88
    character sketch 36, 37
    frontispiece 33–35
Lupton, Christina 67

MacNeil, Denise Mary 70, 72
marriage 10, 56, 69, 74, 81
    polygamy 37–39, 54
    racial intermarriage 58
Marryat, Frederick
    Masterman Ready 1, 35
Marzec, Robert 14
masculinity 3, 11, 28, 30, 37, 62, 63, 69, 72, 73,
    78, 79, 80, 81, 82, 97
    imperial masculinity 7, 9, 10, 13, 19, 21,
      22, 23, 25, 27, 31, 35, 47, 66, 83, 84, 87, 98
masquerade 32, 38, 39, 42, 71, 80–83
matrilineality 73, 76, 82
Maurer, Shawn Lisa 96
McMaster, Juliet 4, 12
McMurran, Mary Helen 72
McQuigge, Alexis 72
Meletinsky, Eleazar 4
Merchant, Peter 50
mimicry 21, 63
miscegenation 54, 58–60, 64
monarch-of-all-I-survey 6, 43, 76, 79, 90
Morris, Ralph
    John Daniel 59–61
mother figure 41, 86, 97
Mr. Robinson Crusoe 28–30
Mücke, Dorothea E. von 5
Munns, Jessica 21
myth 3, 4, 10, 53, 82, 84

Napier, Elizabeth 12, 14, 22
Neville, Henry
    The Isle of Pines 54
New Adam, the 2, 4, 9, 10, 33, 35, 37, 42–45,
    85, 88
noble savage, the 25
Novak, Maximillian 6, 9, 12, 14, 30, 82

O'Malley, Andrew 2, 4
Other, the 1, 13, 21, 28, 46, 50, 60, 64
Ovid
    Metamorphoses 10
Owen, C. M. 68, 71, 72

Paget, Walter 26, 27, 30
Paltock, Robert
    Peter Wilkins 2, 10, 46, 48–67, 82, 84,
      90, 91
    and imperialism 66
    character sketch 56–57
    illustrations 50–53, 56, 58, 66, 67
passions 12, 13, 46–47, 82, 88
patrilineality 59, 66, 76, 78–79
Pearl, Jason H. 49–50
Petit, Susan 88
Picart, Bernard 16, 18, 19, 22, 23
Pick, Daniel 9
Pine, John 16, 17, 22, 23, 25, 28, 31
primitivism 28–30, 36, 37, 42, 44, 46, 47
Providence 13, 31, 41, 45, 46
Prower, Siegbert 3–4

race 21, 50, 59, 60, 66, 72–74, 82, 90
racism 8, 20, 30, 35, 46, 60
Rees, Christine 49
Reilly, Matthew 77
Richards, Penny 21
Richetti, John 2, 3, 23
Riquet, Johannes 15, 54
Robinsonade, the
    and imperialism 1–4, 6, 9, 43, 47, 64, 69,
      70, 84, 90
    as a colonial fantasy 1, 2, 30, 50, 83
    definition 1, 6, 9
    female castaways 10, 62, 68–83, 94–97
    progressive message 2, 3, 9, 47, 50, 63,
      70, 72, 84, 98
    the counter-canonical Robinsonade 3,
      84–98
    the Victorian Robinsonade 1, 13, 25,
      35, 85
Rogers, Woodes 7
Romanticism 48, 49
Rønning, Anne Birgitte 69
Rousseau, Jean-Jacques 31

Sambrook, James 49, 50
Samson, Barney 30
satire 32, 49, 71
Schmidgen, Wolfram 14–15, 46
Selkirk, Alexander 7
sensuality 43, 44, 49, 53, 54, 55, 56, 58, 77,
    86, 87, 91

INDEX

sexuality 6, 10, 12, 30, 37, 54, 69, 93, 96
Shakespeare, William
  The Tempest 35
Silvani, Roman 94
Skonieczny, Krzysztof 87, 88
Smollett, Tobias 48
social programming 1, 3, 25, 30, 47
Stacpoole, Henry De Vere
  Blue Lagoon 10
Starr, G. A. 4
Sterne, Laurence
  Tristram Shandy 12, 66–67
Stimpson, Brian 6, 77
Stothard, Thomas 23, 25
subversion 3, 11, 19, 63, 66, 68, 69, 76, 83, 84, 88, 89, 96, 98
Swenson, Rivka 32, 33
Swift, Jonathan
  Gulliver's Travels 32, 33, 45, 46, 48, 49

The Female American 2, 10, 68–83, 84, 94, 95, 96, 97
  and imperialism 73, 80
  character sketch 73, 74, 82
  illustration 74, 75
The Female Soldier; Or, The Surprising Life and Adventures of Hannah Snell 71

Tokarczuk, Olga
  The Tender Narrator 90, 93
  "Wyspa" 3, 6, 10, 84, 89–93
Tournier, Michel
  Vendredi 3, 40, 84, 85–89, 90, 91
travel writing 5, 33, 57

Uściński, Przemysław 70
utopia 7, 49, 50, 62, 71, 80

Verne, Jules 35, 90, 93
  The Mysterious Island 1, 7–9, 27, 86

Wahrman, Dror 63, 71
Watt, Ian 7, 84, 85
Weaver-Hightower, Rebecca 1, 6–7, 14, 15, 21, 28, 31, 35, 37, 60, 89
Wheeler, Roxann 22, 58
Wheelwright, Julie 71
Wigston Smith, Chloe 70, 80, 82
William Bingfield 46
Wyeth, N. C. 27–28, 29, 30, 47
Wyss, Johann David
  The Swiss Family Robinson 1, 62

Zemeckis, Robert
  Cast Away 30

Printed in the United States
by Baker & Taylor Publisher Services